Family
Ministry

edited by
Gloria Durka
and
Joanmarie Smith

Winston Press

Cover and book design: Maria Mazzara

Library of Congress Catalog Card Number: 80-51106
ISBN: 0-86683-762-0 (previously ISBN: 0-03-057844-2)

Printed in the United States of America
5 4 3 2

Winston Press, Inc., 430 Oak Grove, Minneapolis, MN 55403

To our godchildren
Susan Cotton Seliger
and
Erik John Durka

Contents

Foreword

Perhaps the publication of a book such as *Family Ministry* is an admission that ministry to youth and children is largely ineffective unless it is exercised in the context of ministry to the family. Unfortunately, catechetical age-level programs and teacher training have often tended to fragment the family rather than channel its energies for both in-house and external ministry.

This book explores both the problems and the possibilities of family ministry. In doing so it does not propose adding one more organization to the parish roster. Instead, its analyses and suggestions, if taken seriously and implemented, would call for a major shift in the way we conceive and structure parish life and ministry and leadership. These essays raise such profound questions as: Wouldn't family ministry be effective in a parish

- if families really would see themselves as called to minister?
- if families were ministering to one another?
- if official leadership would recognize that each Christian is by definition called to minister, to share his or her gifts and to receive the gifts of others?
- if lay ministry were understood as being the result of much more than simply communicating information to "uninformed" laity?
- if lay ministry were understood as more than participation in liturgical or catechetical roles and would also include the sharing of one's gifts with society at large and not only within the confines of a

church community?
- if official leadership would so structure activities and relationships within parishes that they would catalyze, foster, and empower lay ministry?

Many of the authors here point out huge problems in the way of making such dreams come true. Dolores Curran, for example, cites hard facts to show that many parishes not only have no family ministry as such but do not even understand what the term means. Lest the reader become discouraged, though, I should point out that both Ms. Curran's essay and many of the other essays in this book offer practical suggestions for solving, with the help of a vital family ministry, the difficulties involved in renewing parish life. I would like to add my own encouraging note by pointing out two educational resources.

First, there is an increasing supply of data available on the experience of parishes throughout the nation that have effectively developed new models of parish as a ministering community. Father Philip Murnion, Executive Director of the U.S. Bishops' Parish Project, is now compiling such data under the sponsorship of the United States Catholic Conference. The pastors of these parishes may be available for consultation with priests and bishops. Planning boards cannot easily find solutions to the organizational crisis of parishes and dioceses, but their task would certainly be lightened if they were to tap the experience of these effective pastors by way of symposiums and consultations.

Secondly, a rich resource for leadership development exists in university programs in Religious Education and Pastoral Ministry. For two decades now, many sisters and brothers and laypersons have embarked upon graduate programs simply for the purpose of enhancing the quality of their own ministry. Some of the best Catholic universities across the country have developed ministry programs that possess the necessary resources to help dioceses develop pastoral leadership. Even without the direct support of diocesan structures, many devoted people, at their own expense, have earned master's degrees at these institutions. If local universities and diocesan planners were to collaborate, how many more effective leaders the Church would have! Unfortunately, many university programs have already been terminated and many dioceses have thereby been impoverished—all because of a failure of cooperation. Universities cannot direct pastoral planning efforts of their own; on the other hand, dioceses can rarely muster the resources necessary for effective high-level leadership train ing. But together, universities and dioceses could be a powerful force for pastoral renewal.

Maurice L. Monette, O.M.I., Ed. D. (Columbia University), is the Director of the Catechetical and Pastoral Institute of Loyola University in New Orleans. His articles have appeared in Adult Education, Catechist, Living Light, PACE, *and* Religious Education.

Preface

In religious education, the next ten years will see, among other things, a new concern for and interest in the family and community. The Roman Catholic bishops, for example, have designated the whole decade of the 1980s as a time for emphasizing this theme. And many agencies and advocacy groups are paying more and more attention to the family. All this signals an important challenge and opportunity for religious educators everywhere.

In this collection we have attempted to surface some of the problems and possibilities of family ministry. In doing so, we have solicited original pieces from persons who have been working in both the theory and the practice of family ministry. Many of the contributors—such as John McCall, Dolores Curran, Gabriel Moran, Maria Harris, and Bernard Cooke—are already well known to religious educators in the field; some are new thinkers who are just emerging; all are well qualified by their experience to address this important topic. The authors include married and single persons, ordained and unordained ministers, members of religious congregations, single and married parents. The Roman Catholic background of many essays is evident, but the authors' presentation of the problems facing family ministry, and the solutions they propose, should be of great help to anyone seriously interested in the field.

While we would be the first to agree that the final word on family ministry is not said here, we are grateful to the contributing authors who in their essays express a new hope for the 80s—family ministry contextualized within a broadened vision of genuine Christian community.

We thank Professor Margaret Jennings of St. Joseph's College, Brooklyn, New York, Professor Bonnie Stevens of the College of Wooster, Ohio, and Cyril A. Reilly of Winston Press for their editorial assistance.

Gloria Durka
Joanmarie Smith, CSJ

Family Ministry

Family Ministry and the Parish: Barriers and Visions

by Dolores Curran

Dolores Curran, author of several family/church-related books, writes a weekly column, "Talks with Parents," which goes into fifty-four diocesan papers and reaches three million readers. Among her many books is Family: Church Challenge for the '80s. *She represented the family at the First Catechetical Congress in Rome in 1971 and more recently served on the Ad Hoc Commission on Marriage and Family which drafted* A Vision and Strategy, *the Plan of Pastoral Action for Family Ministry.*

In this essay, after describing some of the obstacles to effective family ministry in the parish today, she presents a vision of what a successful family ministry could look like.

The Present Situation

Last year when I was invited to compile a resource of models of successful family ministry operating in parishes around the country, I expected some searching, but I was unprepared for the results. I was assigned a researcher, and our first task was to pinpoint parishes that had ongoing and effective programs in one or more of the areas specified by the Plan of Pastoral Action for Family Ministry: Premarrieds and Singles, Married Couples, Parents, "Developing" Families, "Hurting" Families, and Leadership Couples and Families.

In addition to contacting nationally known specialists in the field of family to inquire about the parishes they dealt with, we called diocesan directors of religious education, superintendents of schools and family life directors, asking them, "Which of your parishes would you designate as models of family ministry in your diocese?"

We were astounded to discover that large numbers of those in diocesan leadership positions directed us, not to parishes with family ministry, but to parishes with successful religious education programs for children. They evidenced what is becoming increasingly obvious to me as our greatest block to developing working family ministry in the decade ahead—*an inability to disassociate family ministry from the religious education of children.*

We anticipated this mentality from the laity, particularly parents, who for generations have been imbued with the religious schooling concept, accepting and believing that if their children receive adequate religious instruction, the family will be sufficiently responsible, responsive, and faithful. But my dismay came from discovering the number of professionals—clergy, religious, and lay—who are responsible for transmitting a vision of family ministry that they themselves do not glimpse.

Let me cite just one example. I spoke at length with a superintendent of schools who was familiar with every mention of family in *To Teach As Jesus Did* and *The National Catechetical Directory.* He told me that he was "sold on family" and that until we "build better families we might as well forget about teaching the catechism." He had offered several in-service days on family for his staff, and he obviously saw himself as the strongest supporter of family ministry in his diocesan hierarchy.

Then he directed me to a parish that "really had it all together, familywise." He spoke in such glowing terms of the family ministry operating in that parish that I anticipated finding a model that would be immensely useful in our resource.

Here is what I found: a parish with a school whose parents (representing about one-third of the parish's elementary children and none of the secondary children) were so frightened of closure because of precarious finances that they worked feverishly together on weekly bingo, bazaars, picnics, and fund-raising affairs of all types. This effort bound them together in a close-knit community not commonly found in parishes. They were friends in a single-minded goal—to keep the school open. They served actively on the parish council, on the parish school board, and on the playground every day. They knew the pastor personally, and he openly supported their efforts.

But where was the family ministry? In checking, I discovered that aside from three annual sacramental preparation courses for parents, there was no family ministry at all. Here is what the parish did not have: parenting education of any kind; sexuality education for children or parents; ministry to the separated and divorced;

family faith enrichment ministry; youth ministry; young adult ministry; ministry to the interfaith married; family communication classes; marriage and family counseling; supportive ministry for the single parent; marriage enrichment; aid for parents in dealing with pressures against family life like drugs, cults, television, over-scheduling, teen alienation, changing attitude of/toward women, and mobility; and programs for the committed single.

Why had the superintendent designated this parish as a model of family ministry? Because he made a judgment common in our Church: *He confused ministry to the parish by the family with ministry to the family by the parish.* This is not rare. Many in leadership positions who should know better judge family ministry by what takes place under specifically parish auspices rather than by what takes place in the home. And they judge it on the basis of a minority of their families—the active, supportive, enthusiastic ones. They don't hear the needs of the fragmented, the unchurched and underchurched, and the hurting families.

My classic example of this attitude comes from a layman, an MRE with several years of religious education leadership in a parish. He wrote in response to an article I published in *U.S. Catholic* calling for a per-head allocation of resources in the parish rather than concentrating the bulk on children between six and fourteen. I listed the many areas of need that could be addressed if there were wider vision and more equitable distribution of resources among parish age groups. He wrote, "What does financial planning for widows have to do with religious education?"

Perhaps this is where we should begin in our efforts toward *introducing a vision of total family ministry* in our parishes: not with the NCD or the Plan of Pastoral Action but with pastors, superintendents, principals, DREs, and other leaders, discussing the implications of a question like "What does financial planning for widows have to do with religious education?" If a master-degreed religious educator with years of experience is so mystified over the relationship, we need to return to Square One.

To be fair, we found many others in our research who had a good grasp of total family ministry in the parish, and we managed to identify 50 parishes that had evidence of good ministries in one area or another, although many were in the early stages and must be followed up on before they can be considered prototypes.

But, depressingly, this is only 50 out of 18,600 parishes in our country. Even if there were triple that 50, it is an insignificant effort in comparison to our religious education effort. Many dioceses could not designate even one parish for us to study in family ministry. Some diocesan officials admitted this with chagrin; others didn't know what we were talking about. Some named parishes which simply had an active marriage encounter group but no other family ministry. Most sent us to parishes with effective religious education for children.

Our research bore out the discouraging findings in the *National Inventory of Parish Catechetical Programs:* 81% of our parishes have no programs for singles; 60% have never had parenthood education of any kind; 74% have no ministry to the divorced/separated; 55% never have marriage and family enrichment programs; 73% have never offered family living and sex education.

The *Inventory* soberly concludes:

When one reviews recent studies such as those by Urie Bronfenbrenner or reads the recent

Carnegie study *All Our Children* and the *National Catechetical Directory*, no doubt is left about the need for family ministry. Personnel must be found and materials produced that respond to the need. In light of the fact, however, that approximately one-half of the nation's parishes will not or cannot budget a salary for DREs and that, after almost 10 years, half of the nation's DREs report they have no role description, many questions are raised about the future survival of family ministry.[1]

Then the *Inventory* poses two basic questions:

Is family ministry envisioned as an ad hoc function responding to a momentary surge in family awareness? Or does it see itself as a ministry which must establish recognition, budget and a clear definition of how it distinctly differs from other ministries?[2]

I suspect that most professionals in the education/ schooling concept of ministry believe it is a temporary thrust while most in the family life/parish/faith community model see it as the basis for the future of the Church. And that dichotomy of vision creates potential tension within the diocese and parish. Budgets and power come into play. Where does the DRE fit? Should there be the development of another professional—the total family minister? Which should have priority in the parish: drug education, or religious education; the fragmented family, or the supportive family; youth ministry, or the school library?

While effectiveness of family ministry must ultimately be tallied in the parish, the current vision is not yet there. It is not even evident on a widespread diocesan level. Our task as catechists and family-life specialists is to foster that vision, first among ourselves through materials such as this book, secondly to planners and publishers, and finally, to all of those on the parish level who must eventually evidence the hopes and vision of a total family ministry in the parish.

I have found that once catechists, pastors, and other parish personnel become aware of the history of the current Church emphasis on family ministry, they have a better vision of the ministry itself. Family ministry is not just another way to get the Good News to the children, with parents as teachers instead of the usual classroom teachers. Neither is it a convenient theme chosen by the bishops upon which we can hang religious-education congresses, episcopal letters, and special fund-raising efforts.

Rather, it is a response to the needs articulated by respondents in the 1976 Call to Action Consultation who asked for much more in family ministry than had been anticipated. Instead of requesting more in the way of religious instruction for children and in fighting abortion, two areas we were led to believe parents would want, 825,000 respondents asked for a myriad of ministries to needs undreamed of in the Catholic family of old. It might be helpful here to reprint the top eight issues in the Family category of the Call to Action Consultation. In order of priority, they are:

1. Support of Family Values
Includes reinforcing the value of the family; more family prayer and worship activities; teaching values, respect, dignity, and self-image; promoting cultural and religious traditions in the home.

2. Family Life Education
Includes parish and diocesan programs in parenting

skills—premarital, marital, and postmarital enrichment; sexuality education for parents and children; aging, handicapped and other special areas.

3. *Divorce*

Making the divorced welcome in our pews and ministering to their special needs.

4. *Communication Skills*

Includes teaching families how to communicate with one another, with a particular emphasis in three areas: husband/wife, parent/teen, and family/church.

5. *Pressures Against Family Life*

Includes helping families deal with television, movies, drugs, music, advertising, alcohol, mobility, affluence, unemployment, and the changing attitudes of women.

6. *Counseling*

This is a call for professional marriage, family, and teenage counseling from our church and/or referrals to counselors in touch with our church's beliefs and morals.

7. *Family Sense of Vocation and Social Witness*

Families asked for help in becoming more compassionate, less materialistic, and more ministering families.

8. *Single Parenting*

This concerns the specific type of parenting that single parenting requires. Respondents did not feel that our church was supportive in this area.[3]

A cursory look at this list of needs tells a parish whether it is ministering to today's family or to that obsolete "good Catholic family" of the past. If over half our marriages are now interfaith marriages and the parish still operates on the presumption that the Catholic family is made up of two Catholic parents, both active in the faith, it is ministering to fewer than half of its families. If it has nothing to offer interfaith couples after the marriage (most parishes give a nod to the interfaith marriage only in pre-marriage instruction—before the problems emerge in marriage), it is missing a prime area of ministry.

If nearly a fourth of our marriages end in divorce and/or remarriage and the parish operates on the presumption that Catholic families do not divorce, it is missing ministry to a significant number of families in the pew. If there is a drug, alcohol, or sexually permissive youth culture in the community and the parish has offered nothing to parents to help deal with these pressures, it is avoiding realistic family ministry.

Family ministry, then, is the umbrella we've given to address means of ministering to family needs that don't presently fall under the category of religious education. And because family needs touch people of all ages, our definition of family is much broader than the usual "parents and school-aged children" generally found in the parish. The widow is still a family worthy of ministry. The single constitutes a family. The couple whose children have grown up and away still require ministry. All of these are members of that family-of-families, the parish.

After studying the responses in the Family category of the Call to Action Consultation, the American bishops authorized the Ad Hoc Commission on Marriage and Family to study the issues and to draw up a process by which the needs, articulated on a national level, could be addressed on the parish level. I served on that Commission, along with forty other family-life directors, specialists, bishops, and clergy. It was chaired by Reverend Donald Conroy of the Family Life Division of the United States Catholic Conference (USCC).

We commissioned papers on the theology and sociology of the family. We studied, listened, drafted, and eventually submitted the Plan of Pastoral Action for Family Ministry, *A Vision and Strategy*, to the bishops in May of 1978. They passed it unanimously and named the year 1980 as the opening thrust of a decade of Church emphasis on family ministry.

Uppermost in the minds of the drafters of the Plan was the constant necessity of listening to families within the parish to determine their real needs before developing parish plans of family ministry. We realized that the priority of needs might vary widely from parish to parish. Ministry to the divorced and alienated is generally more urgently needed in metropolitan areas, for example, while rural areas often need more options in family counseling, parent/teen communication, and marriage enrichment. Family cultural and religious traditions are more abundant in ethnic areas, so "a return to religious traditions in the home" which placed high in the national list of family priorities may not come high in such parishes.

We were aware, too, that our parishes do not have a history of listening to the needs of their families and that parishes need to be taught how to listen. A pastoral listening and planning workbook, appropriately titled *Sounds of the Family*, was issued by the USCC in 1978 with suggestions for ways of developing listening techniques, leadership couples, and parish timetables.

Many dioceses and parishes have already initiated efforts to address the needs of their families. Others are ignoring family ministry or are blocked by parish factors that are as varied as they are surmountable. I want to discuss some, but surely not all, of these barriers commonly found in parishes that resist tangible programs of family ministry.

Barriers to Family Ministry

Lack of pastoral vision. One cannot address the vision of family ministry without examining first the vision of the leader of the parish family, the pastor. If his sense of pastoral responsibility to the parish has not changed from what he learned in seminary twenty-five to fifty years earlier, he will be unable to lead his parish family into an appreciation of the vision. If, on the other hand, he has kept himself aware of both the changing family and changing vision of parish through reading, symposiums, pastoral inservice training, familiarity with documents, and workshops in modern ecclesiology, he will be capable not only of listening to the needs in his parish family circle but of transmitting to his parish family both vision and strategy in meeting those needs. That the pastoral role is crucial is attested to by The Papal Committee for the Family in its paper "The Family in the Pastoral Activity of the Church":

> One notes overall an awareness of the need to prepare priests in a serious manner for this pastoral ministry in the service of the family. Too often priests are formed in seminaries for a ministry to individuals, independently of their social milieu. It is necessary to help priests to be more attentive to the family as a social unit, and to the place of each of its members in the evangelical renewal of the family as the first milieu of life.[4]

Failure to transmit a sense of shared ministry. Even when the pastor has a keen vision of family ministry, he often fails to transmit a sense of shared ministry to his parish family. To his people and to himself, old parish formulae operate: "church" problems belong to Father, and "home" problems belong to the parents. Already overwhelmed by the myriad of parish responsibilities and frustrated by insufficient time and energy to meet all the needs himself, this pastor envisions family ministry as an unreachable dream. Sometimes the pastor has a strong understanding of both family ministry and shared ministry but is unable to overcome past conditioning in his parishioners, who nod to it in document but do not respond in actuality, so he gives up and finds it easier to try to do it all himself.

Failure to share the vision of the parish as faith community. John Westerhoff III makes a rational appeal for returning to the goal of Church as faith community over Church as educational institution in his *Will Our Children Have Faith?*

Faith cannot be taught by any method of instruction; we can only teach religion. We can know about religion, but we can only expand in faith, act in faith, live in faith. Faith can be inspired within a community of faith, but it cannot be given to one person by another. Faith is expressed, transformed, and made meaningful by persons sharing their faith in an historical, tradition-bearing community of faith. An emphasis on schooling and instruction makes it too easy to forget this truth. Indeed, the schooling-instructional paradigm works against our necessary primary concern for the faith of persons. It encourages us to teach about Christian religion by turning our attention to Christianity as expressed in documents, doctrines, history, and moral codes.[5]

There is a distinct difference between a faith community and an educational institution. We have great numbers of religiously educated adults without faith. Prolonged emphasis on the primacy of the classroom and of content over the home and faith results in parental feelings of inadequacy and in lack of resources for family ministry, family counseling and family education, and it cements the idea that religion is a subject learned in a class rather than a faith experienced in life.

Thus it is understandable why the American Roman Catholic bishops chose not family alone but a triad of emphases for the 80s, each dependent upon the success of the other: family, evangelization, and parish renewal. It almost seems as if the Holy Spirit brought the three to prominence and popularity simultaneously so that we could visualize their mutual dependency. Until the family is healthy, it is not free to renew the parish. Until the family and parish are evangelized, they will not be empowered to minister to one another. Until the parish addresses its hunger for spirituality, it will not seek evangelization.

Lack of an understanding of the changing sociology of the Catholic family. It is fair to say that the typical Catholic parish is ministering to a family which no longer exists, i.e., "the good Catholic family" of the past which had as its hallmarks:

- two parents
- both parents Catholic
- weekly attendance at Mass, sacraments, and religious instruction
- parish-centered life
- breadwinning father, at-home mother
- strong control of moral influences on children

- relatively controlled pace of life
- criterion of success: whether or not the children grow up to remain Catholic

Statistics tell us that this family no longer exists in large numbers. A conservative estimate points out that one fourth of our marriages end in divorce, nearly half are interfaith, only half of our Catholics regularly attend Mass, confessions have dropped dramatically, and so has attendance at religious education. Family life is not parish centered but community centered. Catholic women are joining the work force as readily as other women. Parents, while still the major child shapers, have strong rivals in media and peers, and the family has lost control of its collective life. Some families never gather for a meal, others only on weekends. Marshall McLuhan remarked that the American family is becoming a public place from which one must escape into a public place for privacy.

Finally, the old criterion for success is no longer valid. Rearing young adults who marry other Catholics and stay in the Church is not the highest priority of Catholic parents today. While it may please them, they place a higher value on rearing grownup children who are not addicted, who see a value in marriage over serial relationships, and who emerge with motivation in life, in contrast to the ambiance of the 60s.

If the Catholic family is significantly different today from what it was twenty-five years ago, it follows that the parish family must offer significantly different services to and by the family. Yet the typical parish remains structurally the same as it was twenty-five years ago. Its organizations for men and women remain primarily social in nature, appeal to the stereotypic old-fashioned—and older—"good" Catholic man or woman (undivorced, non-working mother, etc.), and get smaller annually.

Until we listen to our families and really hear what they tell us—those who are in the pew on Sunday and those who are not—we will not know the makeup of the family to which we are ministering. Do we know how many committed singles we have and what their needs are? Do we know how many older couples are sitting in our pews feeling they have failed their church and their God because their grown children no longer go to Mass on Sunday? How do we minister to a variety of people in our parish family?

Failure to promote a vision of the interrelatedness of catechesis and family life, and failure to convince parents of their primacy in fostering faith. These are linked barriers to family ministry in the parish. Although parent involvement in sacramental preparation is now a reality in over half our parishes, it should be but a prelude to creating an ongoing faith environment in the home. To many parents, there simply isn't any relation between what their children learn in religion class and what goes on in their daily lives. Yet they sense a need for those very skills necessary to internalize God and the Good News on a family level: family communication skills, parenting courses, television control workshops, control of family life, a sense of vocation as a family, help in offsetting peer influences. When the family is so focused inwardly on its own pain and inability to achieve a sense of family, it cannot focus outwardly on God's love and God's gifts to the parish family. Children and parents must love themselves before they can love each other, pewmates, or God.

The Denver mother who said at a Call to Action hearing that she couldn't get concerned about what her thirteen-year-old was not learning in religion class because he hadn't talked to anyone in the family for three weeks had a sense of the interrelatedness of catechesis and family life. We must do a better job of promoting the idea to our families that parenting, communication, sexuality education, marriage enrichment, and harmonious family life are as catechetical in nature as catechisms, doctrines, and classrooms.

Similarly we need to gather together the impressive data showing that the parent is the primary determinant of a person's faith and present it over and over in every way possible until we convince parents of its validity. Until we do so, parents will continue to visualize themselves as adjuncts to the faith process. Adjuncts do not necessarily become responsible.

Reluctance to accept the myriad of needs in today's family as areas of authentic church ministry. We need to redefine authentic ministry in the parish. Is it primarily visitation of the sick, burial of the dead, education of the children, and support of the Church? In many parishes it is. If we add, as areas of authentic ministry, family and parenting education, alienation, empty-nest syndrome and the like, we will be opening ourselves to more training, meetings, and responsibilities. Sometimes it's just easier to ignore needs even when they are preventing our other programs from succeeding. At other times, our own vision of ministry is locked into an earlier Church.

Failure to address uncomfortable issues which come to rest in the family. These are subjects like contraception, the changing role of women, sexuality education, divorce/remarriage, premarital sex, and increasing moral permissiveness. While the family feels baffled in dealing with these subjects, it gets little help from the parish because of the discomfort and possible controversy involved. Only one out of eight children, for instance, gets any kind of sexuality education from his or her parents; yet few parishes offer help in this area to parents or children. Ministry to the separated/divorced, while long a felt need among pastors, has been neglected because it implied approval. Parents who were reared in a Church that taught the sinfulness of the backless formal and the French kiss are trying to counsel teens who exist in a sexually permissive society, without help from their Church. Because of the volatile rhetoric of the women's movement, few parishes have addressed the issue of support of the working woman, day-care centers, or changing awareness that is bringing about tension in marriage. If a family ministry is to succeed, it must address the uncomfortable and controversial needs as well as the comfortable ones.

Failure to generate a family-to-family style of ministry. When a pastoral team—pastor, associates, DRE—considers additional ministries or responsibilities in the parish, it tends to view them in relation to its ability to implement them rather than in relation to the ability of the total parish to meet new needs. Implicit in the Plan of Pastoral Action for Family Ministry is the belief that the capability for this ministry already exists in untapped gifts in the pew. Laity are uniquely suited for family ministry, but we must open that giftedness to the laity themselves. We must give them permission to view themselves as ministers. Interestingly, this coincides with the seventh area of need as expressed in the Call to Action Consultation: Families asked for help in becoming more compassionate, less materialistic, and more ministering.

In a paper she delivered at the Atlanta Call to Action Hearing on Family, in August, 1975, Rosemary Haughton referred to the need of family to be ministers:

> Contrary to popular belief, the best marriages and the happiest families don't happen because people concentrate first of all, on the quality of their relationships, but rather when the couple and then the family as a whole is involved in something bigger. . . .

So, paradoxically, one of the needs can become the solution: a need to minister—a need for ministers. I know a sister who set up an adult tutorial program which was based on a one-to-one educational model. She invited adults from educated suburban parishes to volunteer to tutor adults from impoverished parishes to help them get their High School Equivalency diplomas. She credits the success of her program, now in its tenth year, to the "need to be needed" by the advantaged. This need is real. She identified an area of ministry where gifts and talents could be utilized in a practical and local manner. In this way, she brought together the needy recipient and the needy giver.

If the parish team members view themselves as agents of development of family ministers rather than as becoming family ministers themselves, they will have glimpsed a vision of what family ministry can and should become.

A homey example is the DRE who heard the pain of a few families who were having difficulty living harmoniously with their teens. She recognized the gifts of one particular couple in the parish who had reared a number of teenagers with good attitudes and with minimal disharmony while doing so, so she asked this couple if they would meet with two other couples and hear their questions and counsel them. "But we don't have any qualification," they replied.

This is a natural response on the part of many effective parents (those whom Toffler referred to as "professional parents"). Because they don't have degrees in human behavior, they feel they have few gifts to offer other parents, particularly in a church setting. But the DRE opened their giftedness to themselves and invited them to alleviate the pain of the other families through listening to their problems and answering their questions. They were immensely helpful and became instrumental in establishing a parish parenting course. The DRE had a fine understanding of her role. She did not attempt to counsel hurting families but used her gifts to develop ministry gifts in others.

These are some of the barriers that loom large in preventing effective family ministry on a parish level. I find that it's a good technique to address them openly in a parish that is studying family ministry. Some will apply to the parish; some may not. But because they are almost universal in nature, they are effective tools to use in initiating discussion.

A Vision of Parish Family Ministry

After we presented the Plan of Pastoral Action for Family Ministry to the Roman Catholic bishops at their May meeting in Chicago, 1978, we were part of the press conference that followed. We were asked a number of questions on various aspects of the Plan, but we apparently were not giving reporters what they really needed to hear. Finally, the religious reporter from the *New York Times* asked me, "If this plan is implemented to your satisfaction, what will the parish be doing in five years that it isn't doing now?"

It was an excellent question and one that might be discussed at the beginning of any parish family ministry effort.

From my experiences on the various commissions preparing for the Year and Decade of the Family in our Church, I have a vision of what I would like to see accomplished on a practical level in the average parish in the next ten years. Here it is.

The parish with total family ministry has an ongoing listening process out of which it develops means and programs to meet the needs it hears. It does not attempt to meet all the needs simultaneously but chooses priority needs in each area of ministry: pre-marrieds and singles; married couples; parents; hurting families; developing families; leadership couples.

The parish with total family ministry has on its staff a professionally trained family minister who is responsible for developing listening structures, training leadership couples and families, counseling marriages and families and developing like-to-like ministry within the parish. This professional is not qualified through volunteer channels but by earning a master's degree in family ministry which includes courses in counseling, family sociology, ecclesiology, and behavioral sciences.

The parish with total family ministry keeps its various ministries in balance: liturgical, educational, and family. It does not view itself first as an educational community but as a faith community. It focuses on three areas: family ministry, evangelization, and parish renewal, constantly evaluating its efforts and devising means of using one to enrich the other.

The parish with total family ministry focuses on developing ministers within the parish to address ministry needs. It promotes the vision that parish family ministry means ministry by parishioners to parishioners. It views its pastoral team as professionals in their area of expertise—spiritual, educational, family—who generate, coordinate, and direct the various shared ministries operating within the parish family.

That is my vision of the parish that ten years from now has successfully implemented our hopes in family ministry. Not exactly Church-shaking. No doubt some of my colleagues have a different vision. I tend to be a pragmatist, focusing too much at times on the reality of parish structures rather than on the dream of what could be.

Still, if the average parish could achieve such a vision and reality of family ministry in the next ten years, I believe we would witness the parish and Church renewal we are seeking.

Notes

1. *A National Inventory of Parish Catechetical Programs* (Washington, D.C.: United States Publications Office, 1978), p. 40.
2. Ibid., p. 41.
3. Unpublished data from the Writing Committee on Family, Call to Action Consultation, 1976.
4. Papal Committee for the Family, *The Family in the Pastoral Activity of the Church* (Washington, D.C.: USCC Publications Office, 1978), p. 10.
5. New York: Seabury Press, 1976, p. 23.

For Further Reading

Conroy, Donald. "Total Family Programming." *Origins* 5, November 13, 1975 (Washington, D.C.: NC Documentary Service).

The Family: Liberty and Justice for All. (Atlanta Hearing, August, 1975.) Washington, D.C.: USCC Publications Office, 1976.

Kenniston, Kenneth, and the Carnegie Council on Children. *All Our Children: The American Family Under Pressure.* New York: Harcourt, Brace, Jovanovich, 1978.

A National Inventory of Parish Catechetical Programs. Washington, D.C.: USCC Publications Office, 1978.

Potvin, Raymond H.; Hoge, Dean R.; Nelson, Hart M. *Religion and American Youth: With Emphasis on Catholic Adolescents and Young Adults.* Washington, D.C.: USCC Publications Office, 1976.

Sounds of the Family: A Pastoral Listening and Planning Workbook. Washington, D.C.: USCC Publications Office, 1978.

A Vision and Strategy: The Plan of Pastoral Action for Family Ministry. Washington, D.C.: USCC Publications Office, 1978.

Westerhoff, John III. *Will Our Children Have Faith?* New York: Seabury Press, 1976.

The Western Family and the Future of the Church. (No. 51.) Brussels: Pro Mundi Vita, 1974.

Family: A Garden of Spices

by Paul Clement Czaja

Paul Clement Czaja is a Research Associate at Fordham University's Graduate School of Religion and Religious Education; he is working on a doctoral dissertation concerned with the spiritual life of families. His previous experience was gained as teacher and headmaster of Whitby School, the American Montessori Center in Greenwich, Connecticut. He and his wife Anita have been sharing life and love together with their four children (now teenagers) here and there over the past eighteen years.

In this essay, drawing on his own family experience, he analyzes the wonderful forces that shape children's lives. At the same time he urges parents not only to appreciate those forces and to watch them intently, but to enter into a real fellowship of growth with their children.

God wants families. Perhaps more than in any other way, he seems to work his hardest at this divine strategy. Where else has he built in so much tenderness at the very beginning? In all my living I have not been as helplessly caught up in loving as I have been in this supremely human venture called family. As far as I am concerned, that is a good sign that God himself is at work. Where there is love and caring, there is God.

Looking back over the years, I find that my best preparation for adult life and parenthood was the time I spent one summer as a young boy growing carrots. It was one of those brief, simple happenings of childhood that stands out somehow throughout all the rest of my life as being the source of the best bit of wisdom ever learned. Shamelessly I confess that except for that stint with carrots I received no other training for the great challenge of making it as a parent in modern Babylon. Yet it was there in that little vegetable garden that my heart first caught fire, that I first seriously became involved as a person, that I first realized that I was in a working partnership with the Almighty God of creation. This essay concerns the truths learned during that apprenticeship and how to apply them as we raise our children within that garden of spices called family. I would hope that people working in family ministry would try to convey at least the gist of my experience to the families they deal with.

In the early 1940s, during World War II, President Roosevelt called on urban America to raise "Victory Gardens" to alleviate the food shortage. So my mother marched my twin brother and me—we were eight years old—down to a flat, trampled-down lot in the Bronx and asked us what vegetable each of us wanted to plant. Since I loved carrots I asked for them, and she poured some little black seeds into my hand. Talk about existentialist angst! Those little black dead things could grow? In that dead, bare dirt?

I hadn't said a word, but my mother was always good at noticing faces. So she assured me that those really were live seeds and they really would grow. I had my private doubts, but I obediently scratched a few lines into the hard-packed dirt, dropped in the tiny black seeds, and muddied up the whole mess by pouring water all over them.

I had no faith, I say, but I did come every day to look. And sure enough, within a week or so—sprouts! Carrot sprouts began breaking out of that hardpan! I cannot tell you what an impact it had on my young life to see the outright miracle of that new life coming out of Bronx dirt, defying despair—life almost in spite of everything. My carrot sprouts were a joyous crowd of light green feathers. They just delighted my heart, and they made me a believer forever.

Granted, my role in that partnership with our God of organic life was not to be compared with his side of it, but I had helped it happen, and I felt a goodly share of God's pride in parenting carrots. More importantly, my intimacy with the joyful happening made me witness something that was superabundantly marvelous: the liberation of life. Somehow what my mother had promised had come true, for within every one of those tiny black seeds there was hidden a force of individual life waiting to be released. In awe I watched and realized what actually was going on there in that humble Bronx garden. A spirit of life within each of those seeds could take in dirt and transform it into that greenness which is a carrot sprout. There was a built-in wisdom that could direct a transubstantiation so that some of the dirt became root, some became leafage, and some actually became delicate flowers. Seeing all that happen was my first wow! And that wow opened me up to all the other wows that have followed to this very day. Something special is going on at the heart of things, and it is wonderful to watch it happening all over the place.

Is not the same thing happening in family? God is at work again, except that instead of carrots it is children and parents. Not only does each person begin life as a seed, but each family begins its superorganic life in the hyphenated simplicity of a Buberesque I-Thou germination. Life ever redoubles into greater life. And all life tends toward a fulfillment that is galactic in its dimensions and power. Looking closely at myself reveals that indeed I am a living galaxy of cells. What began as a single cell of matter has been nourished and directed from within and from without to become all kinds of cell systems which wondrously hang together to make me me. I am billions of cells, and I am organized, and I move, and do more—much, much more. This galaxy of cells that is me knows and reflects and speaks and loves and takes part in the great partnership of ever-new creating.

One day one of my cells out of the billions of them, a seed cell, left my galactic body, crossed some space, and entered deep within that friendly galaxy that is my wife, to unite with just one of her earth cells. And that became our son David! Then another was sent from deep to deep and became our son Christian, another our daughter Claudia, and another our youngest son, Jonathan. Out of all the billions, just four cells of mine and four cells of my wife have made a miraculous leap from simple unicellular life to become those spectacular island universes called human beings. Galaxies embraced, kissed, mixed matter a bit, and the unbelievable outcome was our children, who know us as mother and father, who speak to us, who love us, who live personal lives together with us that are gifted now to be infinite, praise God!

All this is staggering. There is such a force at work in all this! And what an awesome accomplishment to end up with the actual creation of persons! There is no ending at all but always a new beginning. Some look at all this going on and say it is only blind chance at work. But I have found the force behind all this creation trustworthy and familiar.

Such an awareness and such a trusting attitude, I believe, have much to do with making family life fulfilling rather than frustrating for parents and children. This awareness and attitude depend on parents' becoming conscious of what is at work there within the phenomena of children. Just as when I long ago first took hold with my mind and heart of the phenomena of carrots, we as parents must come to know the reality of the person-processes of our children. Like carrots, our children are organic and grow from the inside out, being nourished by simple elements provided generously. And so the most basic thing we must do as parents if we are going to be genuine in our relationship to our children is to really observe them. This is not easy to do, for we have grown so busy that we hardly see what is going on around us. And even when we hold still long enough to begin to see, we have such a strong habit of remaining up there with all our thoughts above our eyebrows that our eyes often stare blankly. Yet if we are going to interact with our children in a respectful way, we must truly observe them.

Once we begin to observe our children we discover three forces leading them toward maturity and fulfillment.

1. The first force is *their overwhelming power and urge to grow:* their dynamic interior power and tendency to reach out and take in nourishment, to develop, to move toward self-fulfillment. The point is that we parents can count on this force. We must have trust enough to sit back and try not to interfere with this self-development. Children are being directed toward a destiny by a wisdom within that is greater than our heady considerations. Our exaggerated concern for our carrot plants should not lead us to dig them up to see what is happening.

2. The second force shaping our children's life is their *social environment:* family, neighborhood, school, church. Like plants that need and respond to the proper environment of soil, water, air, and sunlight, children need a healthy social environment if they are to grow. Among those many environmental factors let us mention just four.

The first of these is *opportunities for purposeful work,* the kind of work that is as *interesting* to children as play is. It need not be play, but it must be genuinely interesting, or it drains their spirit of life. Tasks are either challenging or they are not. So parents must always watch for the display of interest on their children's faces as they go about their tasks within the home, neighborhood, school, or church environment. Their faces will tell if their activity is earthy enough for them to sink roots.

A second environmental factor that children need and respond to is *informal, friendly relationships* within a lively community. Just as every living thing requires water to keep the minerals moving, so children need and respond to the natural flow of interpersonal dynamics to get their psychic juices going full stream. I grew up within a school system in which all the desks were screwed down in rows, and my hand was struck with a ruler every time I spoke to the child across from me. Thank God for life within the streets; otherwise my personality would now surely be stunted. The best model for us is the natural structure of family life, where we find a mixture of sizes and ages and types moving in and out of private and social time fairly harmoniously. Children, because they are people, need and respond to streams of living water that are found in intimacy and lively friendships.

A third social environmental factor that children need and respond to is the subtle one of *respect for their individuality*. The most striking aspect of children is that each one is unique, incomparable. Yet they find themselves being compared one to another much too often within the home and especially within the school. Grading children as if they were nonpersons—"second graders" or "third graders"—is simply disrespectful. Ranking them as first, second, or last within these arbitrary structures is patently disgraceful. Saying things such as "Why can't you be more like your brother!" is just plain silly. Children have been gifted each with their own faces, their own birthdays, their own talents, their own styles, their own purposes. There is nothing to compare. We can clearly see this if we would only be so kind as to notice. Respect for individuality is the essential atmosphere needed for personal freedom.

The fourth and final social environmental factor that children need and react to is *some specific response from a person who cares*. The word *specific* is important. Let me retell an old story to illustrate what I mean by a specific response. When Alexander the Great had been great long enough to feel thankful, he decided to return to his childhood village and pay homage to a fondly remembered teacher. Upon entering the poor adobe home he found his old teacher sitting in the bathtub, happy and warm in the morning's sun. With all his entourage behind him, Alexander came close, greeted his old master, and asked what he could do to honor him. The old man looked up and asked Alexander to move a little to the left, for he was casting a shadow across his naked wet body and causing a chill. In his anxiety to please, Alexander had missed noticing the gooseflesh forming on his master's shoulder and so had missed a chance at making a specific response.

3. The third force of life is *the call to personal excellence*. Like the immense gravitational pull of the moon and sun and stars that never lets the oceans rest, this mysterious power keeps drawing us away from the earthly, from the mundane, to the unknown beyond. We are a haunted people, ever dreaming, ever yearning to get free of the bonds of matter, to enter new realms of being, to create and to be part of what has never yet been known on earth. And so we often find ourselves imagining and praying. The occurrences of imagination and prayer are like tides pulling our spirit out and away, evoking self-sacrifice and heroism. And how else can we explain our sense of hope when we are up against the bleakest of circumstance? And what of that sense of humor which brings laughter even before the tears have dried? We are God's "peculiar people," as Scripture says, a people called and gifted from afar. We hardly know what to make of ourselves, but we rejoice in our awareness that we are being called to something more. Children of all ages yield much more easily to this pull than we who have grown heavy in our ways, and so we parents are directed to notice that the Kingdom of Heaven is theirs already, in the here and now, and that we had best join in with them.

This essay has urged parents to observe intently the

wonderful God-given forces that are shaping their children—forces that answer their deepest needs and bring their children to rich maturity and self-fulfillment.

But parenting means more than just *watching* the garden grow. After all, as I learned back there in the Bronx, the experience of gardening affected me as much as it did my carrots. It was a sort of fellowship that shaped gardener as well as carrots.

Family life is like that: a *fellowship* in the deepest sense of the word; not the superficial "fellowship" that happens at any casual get-together, but a fellowship denoted by the ancient Greek word *koinonia*, which meant "having things in common." Now, what we parents have most in common with our children is our *mutual* commitment to expanding life, a fellowship in which parents and children *help one another* to grow and to find fulfillment.

How good it is to know that the God who planted the first garden and put the human family in charge of it is still watching over it and us, still giving life and growth and full development to that garden and that family!

The Christian Family as Moral Educator: Possibilities and Limitations

by John L. Elias

John L. Elias, Ed. D., is Associate Professor of Adult Education and Educational Psychology in the Graduate School of Religion and Religious Education, Fordham University. His publications include Psychology and Religious Education *and* Philosophical Foundations of Adult Education. *He and his family reside in New Jersey.*

Christian families, like all families, have a powerful influence on the moral development of children. John Elias shows how theory and research in psychology, sociology, and anthropology have established this influence. Drawing from these same disciplines, he also points to the limitations of the family in the area of moral development. He maintains that family educators and ministers need to be aware of both possibilities and limitations.

Commonsense wisdom tells us that the family is an extremely important agency for the moral development of children. This wisdom arises from our experience that our own deepest values and those of the people we have observed were formed in the earliest years in the family. Hence we most often turn to family influences to explain both good and bad character and behavior. For the most part we believe that delinquents come from less desirable family environments and that good persons come from good home environments.

This commonsense knowledge of family influence has been reinforced through religious teachings and literature that have emphasized the family's importance in transmitting and inculcating moral and religious values. Parents have often been told that they are responsible for the religious and moral upbringing of their children and that Christian values can be maintained in society only if these values are taught in the home.

Educators, too, have supported this commonsense wisdom. They have contended that the work of the school in the areas of values and attitudes training will not be effective unless moral values and attitudes have been developed within the home. In such sensitive areas as sex education, schools have often decided that all that they can do is impart knowledge; they must leave the teaching of moral values to families.

Though our common sense tells us that families are important in moral development, our experience, observation, and reflection make it clear that peers, schools, churches, friendships, and other influences are also important. Moreover, without denying the family's great influence, we should also realize the family's limitations in this area. Hence this essay will address both those aspects.

In the past forty years, researchers in psychology, sociology, and anthropology have studied the family's influence in the moral development of children and youth. This essay will examine their research in order to determine the nature of that influence and the processes by which it occurs. We should note that although the evidence in this highly complex field is not scientifically conclusive, it is strong enough to support our commonsense understanding of both the strength and the limitations of the family's influence on moral development. Our examination of the evidence should be useful to all who are working in a religiously based family ministry.

The Family as a Primary Agent of Socialization

The process by which we all learn the values and norms of our society so that we can function effectively within that society is called socialization. We usually apply the term to children and adolescents, but increasingly we are speaking of adult socialization to indicate that the process continues throughout life.

We are socialized through many agencies, especially families, schools, churches, and the media. The family is called a primary group of socialization—one of those groups which, according to Cooley, are

> characterized by intimate face-to-face association and cooperation. These groups are primary in several senses but chiefly in that they are fundamental in forming the social nature and ideals of the individual. . . . These groups involve the sort of sympathy and mutual identification for which 'we' is the natural expression.[1]

Besides the family, other primary groups include a

play group, school friends, a teenage group or gang, and a work group. Of all these groups, however, the family presents the best opportunities for socialization, because children are members of families during their most formative years, and families often provide the most enduring interpersonal relationships.

Socialization takes place within the family because children so identify with the family as a group that its ways become part of their own selves. The family is the first reference group whose values, norms, and practices one assimilates and uses to evaluate the values, norms, and behaviors of others. The patterns of interaction that children see within the family become models for their own interactions with others.

Though all families socialize in moral values and norms, it is clear from research that there are different kinds of families and that these differences are important in the socialization of values. Gans has described three types of families: adult-centered families that are run by adults for adults; child-centered families that are more attentive to children; and adult-centered families that place a great emphasis on self-development and individual growth of all their members, parents and children alike.[2] Baumrind has found similar family patterns. The authoritarian family is parent dominated; the permissive family is child dominated. The authoritative family, however, is characterized by an interactive relationship in which forces exerted by the parents and children are in a healthy state of tension. This latter pattern seems to produce the highest levels of competency and responsibility in children, as both observation and teacher reports indicate.[3]

The importance of the family in the teaching of values has also been confirmed by studies that have investigated the effects of schooling on young people. The studies of both Greeley and Jencks, which include reviews of many other studies, have shown that the learning of religious and school-related values is strongly related to home influences.[4]

But theory and research also indicate the limitations of the family in the area of moral development. In Durkheim's view it is not the family but the school that can provide the moral education that a society needs for its young members. In his basically theoretical and not empirically based study, he contends that the atmosphere of love, sympathy, and understanding in the home does not provide the strong context for the disciplined behavior needed in society.[5] Bronfenbrenner and others have further contended that the family is losing out to the peer group in influencing the moral standards of the young. Bronfenbrenner sees this as a harmful situation which is found increasingly in many industrial countries.[6] The study by the President's Panel on Youth, headed by the sociologist James Coleman, also asserted that in the United States the influence of parents has waned and that of peer groups and media has increased.[7]

It must be noted, too, that family influence on moral development can be seriously affected by changes and disruption in society. Geiger's report on the effects of social upheaval and civil strife in Russia from 1919 to 1929 observed that great numbers of uncared-for youngsters roamed the streets and engaged in crimes and violent actions. A strong collective education under Makarenko, the father of modern Russian education, was the solution to this problem of general social disorientation.[8]

What the research on socialization and moral development within the family tells us is that we must avoid the two extremes of idealizing the family as the sole determiner of moral development of children and youth, and rejecting the family as an important force in moral development. The moral development of the young begins in the family, but it certainly does not end there. More can be done to help families provide an atmosphere for healthy moral development. Some indications of theories in this area will be explored later in this essay. But in the area of moral development we must be aware of the limitations of the family due to its social nature and due to the many social forces that impinge upon it.

By nature the family, like any social institution, best socializes its members to values which are necessary for its own survival. Families tend to mediate the values of the other institutions of society in such a way that those values will reinforce family values. Thus parents want schools and churches to reinforce the values of the home. Much criticism of schools and churches by parents comes from the perceived failure of those institutions to reinforce family values. Debates over integration, sex education, progressive religious education, and suitable reading materials in school indicate the basic conservative and protective feature of family demands. This is not to say that all families are opposed to all proposed changes. But the conflicts of values in these areas indicate that moral development and education is a complex matter involving the rights of individuals, families, schools, churches, the local community, and the broader society.

Family Influence in Psychological Processes of Moral Development

Psychological theory and research have made important contributions in the area of moral development. In the past thirty years various theories have attempted to explain how the young develop their values. Prominent theories include behaviorism, social learning theory, psychoanalytic theory, cognitive developmental theory, and personalist-existential theory. In this short essay it is not possible to adequately treat even the salient features of the research. (A full treatment can be found in Derek Wright's *The Psychology of Moral Behavior.*[9]) Rather, I will comment on the particular *process* or processes that each theory considers to be fundamental in explaining moral development; I will also discuss how those processes are relevant to the family as moral educator.

According to behaviorism, *reinforcement* of behavior is the fundamental process of moral development. In this view moral learning is reduced to learning moral behavior. Desired behavior is shaped by suitable rewards and by structuring the environment so that desired behaviors can be more easily shaped. Though some behaviorists see a role for punishment in eliminating undesired behaviors, Skinner maintains that it is ineffective and that only positive and non-punitive reinforcements should be used.[10] In his view undesirable behavior should never be reinforced, neither by attention nor by punishment; it should simply be ignored.

The process of reinforcement certainly takes place in family moral training, especially in the earliest years. Parents determine what is right and wrong for their children by the actions they praise and the actions they blame or punish. Through these processes correct moral behaviors are developed. In a religious context the principle of reinforcement is appealed to by placing religious rewards or punishments before the children. One of the values of

Skinner's work on reinforcement is that it makes clear some of the processes that have been operative in religious moral training, with its appeals to the rewards of heaven and God's love and the punishment of hell and God's wrath.

Within a limited scope it is hard to quarrel with the behaviorist's basic idea that behavior is shaped by reinforcement. But this theory cannot explain all forms of moral learnings and development. By not attending to awareness and other mental processes, it presents a mechanistic view of human behavior in which there is some kind of automatic response to an act of reinforcement. Yet experience with such programs as behavioral modification shows a significant drop in behavior change in persons who leave the controlled situation.

The processes of moral development proposed by psychoanalytic theory are *identification* and *internalization*. Freud explains these processes in this manner. Young children experience many frustrations, some due to parental control and others due to such factors as illness and physical discomfort. These frustrations create hostility towards parents. In order not to lose the love of parents, children repress this hostility by identifying with their parents and their parents' behavior. They then experience guilt feelings when they do things that they know their parents will disapprove. They attempt to avoid these guilt feelings by acting in accordance with the incorporated and internalized parental prohibitions. Freud describes these parental prohibitions in his concept of the superego.[11]

Psychoanalytic theories of moral development are much concerned with intra-family dynamics. These theories hold that the relationships between members of one's family become part of one's moral system. Persons will develop split moral personalities if they view their parents as divided and antagonistic. An ambivalent moral system will result if individuals are confronted with contradictory demands within the family. Thus in psychoanalytic theory, as developed after Freud, one identifies not only with the parent of the same sex but also with the very family system and the relationships that exist within the family.

Identification and internalization theories have been criticized on a number of counts. It is clear that children do not identify with all the characteristics of parents but with the more external ones. There is also evidence that parent identification wanes as persons come under the influence of other significant individuals and groups. Stanley Milgram's studies have shown how readily people can go against their professed values.[12]

Notwithstanding certain criticisms made against this theory, it does indicate some important features of moral development. Values that are internalized in the family situation are formative, even though they may also be reversible through powerful outside influences. Internalization of values may be followed by a time of personal testing, but there should be values upon which this testing develops.

In its practical implications this theory has given mixed signals. In the hands of A. S. Neil, the theory has encouraged a permissive and almost amoral approach to child rearing.[13] On the other hand, Bruno Bettelheim argues out of this tradition for a stringent morality based on fear and trembling.[14] Neil argues that children must from the earliest years be free to develop as autonomous persons, and that to become such they must not be presented with moral norms. Bettelheim, however, believes that immediate pleasure must be postponed in order to gain more lasting satisfaction. In Bettelheim's view a powerful reality principle must check the harm that the pleasure principle can do to a person's moral development.

Neil's approach to moral education is unrealistic for the needs of individuals and society, but I fear that Bettelheim's proposal will only lead to more patients for his psychoanalytic profession. Identification and internalization are powerful forces to be reckoned with in moral development. Families cannot handle moral development either by denouncing responsibility or by imposing a too-stringent morality. A balanced view means looking to all the processes, agencies, and forces that are operative in the moral development of children.

In their theory of moral development, social learning theorists have stressed primarily the process of *modeling*. Through this theory they have attempted to combine the best features of reinforcement theory and identification-internalization theory. The most thorough research in the area of modeling has been done by Albert Bandura, who observes:

> Most human behavior is learned observationally through modeling and observing others. Through modeling one forms an idea of how new behaviors are performed and on later occasions this coded information serves as a guide for action.[15]

According to modeling theory, modeling involves a number of sub-processes: attending to the behavior of others, retaining this in mind through symbolic or coded forms, and reproducing the behavior under proper motivation. Modeling theory has been used to explain how people develop styles of thinking, reasoning, and judging.

Bandura contends that children tend to adopt their model's moral standards. Nevertheless, he sees modeling as only part of the process. In the early stages of life, external control is necessary. But as children grow older, social sanctions should replace physical ones. After moral standards of conduct are established by modeling and instruction, foreseen consequences should serve as deterrents to transgressive actions. According to modeling theory not only parents but also other adults, peers, and symbolic models play influential roles in moral development. In fact the theory proposes exposure to various modeling situations as the way to promote mature moral development.

It is clear, then, that both reinforcement and identification-internalization processes are involved in modeling. All of these processes are involved in the discussion of family discipline by such learning theorists as Hoffman.[16] In a number of research studies Hoffman and others have found that the use of power-assertion discipline by parents seems to produce weak moral development. Moral development is described in this view as including processes of identification and internalization, the development of internal and not external moral orientation, guilt over transgression, acceptance and denial of blame, and altruism or consideration for others. These researchers have also found that indirect, psychological, love-oriented discipline, exercised either through love withdrawal or induction of the correct behavior, seems to foster strong moral development. Punishment has been found to be an ineffective means of moral training, for it gives a model of anger and resentment for children to imitate. What is preferable, in this view, is a discipline based on empathy induced in the child by making use of the child's natural proclivities toward empathy and consideration for others.

The research on modeling is extensive and attempts to account for many of the factors of moral development. To summarize: The findings emphasize the role of parents but not to the exclusion of other factors. Proper modeling demands great consistency between what one says and what one does. Care must also be taken that children truly internalize the values that are modeled; otherwise they might quickly change values upon meeting models with contrary values.

In its approach to moral development and education, cognitive-developmental theory places primary emphasis on the process of *moral reasoning* and on inducing *cognitive conflict*. The chief proponents of this view, Jean Piaget and Lawrence Kohlberg, contend that growth in moral reasoning ability makes the critical difference in moral development. Piaget identifies two stages in children's moral development. In the heteronomous stage they judge the rightness or wrongness of their actions in terms of the damage done. In the autonomous stage, after the age of seven, they begin to make moral judgments on the basis of the intent of the doer. The first stage features respect for and obedience to adult authority. The second stage is an adult stage of regard for others and cooperation with them.[17]

Kohlberg agrees with Piaget as to the basic process of learning in general and moral learning in particular. He sees all learning as taking place through the interaction of the individual with the environment. Kohlberg has devised a theory wherein there are three levels of morality: pre-conventional, conventional, and post-conventional or principled morality. In each level there are two stages. Through a process of moral reasoning children pass from rigid external reasoning about punishment and egoistic concerns to the acceptance of the conventional standards of society, and finally in some cases at adult life, to internal standards and internal motivation. Cross-cultural research done by Kohlberg and his associates establishes the fact that the stages are universal and develop in an unvarying sequence.[18]

As can be expected, such claims by cognitive developmentalists have not escaped criticism.[19] Many consider the theory too cognitively oriented and inattentive to other important factors in moral development. The empirical basis for the theory has also been questioned. Moreover, the theory does not adequately explain why some develop and others do not. Philosophers see the theory as basically unclear in its definitions of moral development and in its understanding of the various stages.

Notwithstanding these criticisms the theory is the one most commonly discussed by educators and psychologists. Religious educators have been especially drawn to it because it emphasizes values such as personal freedom, responsibility, conscience, justice, rights, and personal relationships and because it rejects cultural relativism. This theory views the human person as capable of developing in the areas of mind and reason. It also clearly distinguishes between the moral development of the child and that of the adult.

Of all the theories thus far considered, the cognitive-developmental theory takes least account of parental and other environmental influences. The environment, and thus the home, is important for Kohlberg insofar as it provides opportunities for role taking. The general availability of these opportunities—rather than specific experiences with parents or experiences of discipline, punishment, and reward—is what promotes moral reasoning. Kohlberg contends:

> With regard to the family, the disposition of parents to allow or encourage dialogue on value issues is one of the clearest determinants of moral stage advance in children. Such an exchange of viewpoints and attitudes is part of what we term 'role taking opportunities.'[20]

Kohlberg's approach to moral development emphasizes the school more than the influence of home and parents. But his approach certainly has relevance for parents. Kohlberg's approach can be helpful as part of any program of religious moral training which pays attention to the quality of moral reasoning and motivation. Parents who want to include the religious dimension in moral development must, however, supplement Kohlberg's ideas on the primacy of justice and moral reasoning with specifically religious motivation and concerns. Kohlberg does not consider the content of moral teaching, only the processes of moral reasoning. A religious content would include the stories, myths, dogmatic and moral teachings, rites, values, and norms of a specific religious tradition.

The final process of moral development to be discussed has been presented by existential, humanistic, or Third Force psychologists. These theorists maintain that moral development comes about chiefly through *existential choice* or *personal valuing*. This view is found in works of

Maslow, Rogers, May, Allport, and Laing. Allport contends that though various factors influence us in making our moral decisions, personal freedom is still the critical element in moral development. Allport here reacts against the determinism of many psychological views which place the human person at the mercy of drives and environment.[21]

The stance taken by these psychologists in favor of freedom is an important one. Although their view does not have the research base to support it that other theories have, it corresponds more to a traditional and commonsense view of the human person and to our commonsense talk about our experience of human freedom. In the view of Rogers, the individual should trust his or her basic instincts about what is valuable. Rogers believes that the valuing process of many adults is faulty, for adults often reflect the values of others rather than choose their own values. He believes that adults should recapture some of the instinctual aspects of the infant's valuing process and should be willing to trust themselves, express negative feelings, and present themselves as real and not posed persons.[22]

Making allowance for some of the lofty romanticism of such views, this approach still seems important in treating the family's involvement in moral development. For it holds that all members of the family, even the youngest, are persons with the right to make choices and to develop as they choose. This view is obviously to be moderated in the case of children and adolescents. But the principle is valid for them also. Parents must ever be questioning what personal values they are consciously or unconsciously inculcating in their children. One can of course make a strong case for transmitting values accepted by one's whole society. But when there are honest differences of opinion on particular moral values and norms, parents must be careful to respect the personal autonomy of the child and lay the groundwork for free choice in later life. Any worthwhile moral education and training must take into account the developing freedom of the child by appealing to evidence for what is taught.

The existentialist-personalist emphasis on freedom is an antidote to more deterministically based theories, but it cannot stand alone as a complete theory of moral development. Especially in its more popularized versions the theory makes freedom too easy a task and does not sufficiently attend to factors which impinge on human freedom—such factors as environment and the more tragic elements of human life.

Family Ministry and Moral Development

Social-science research indicates that the family's role as moral educator is important but limited. It is interesting that Christian tradition and history agree with that view. Christianity has recognized that there can be conflict between membership in a particular family and membership in a Christian community, that the family can either help or hinder one's full development as a Christian person. A realistic family ministry will honestly face the tensions of this dual membership.

According to Sidney Callahan the conflict between family membership and church membership arises primarily

> because Christianity emphasizes the absolute worth of each individual, regardless of social status, and at the same time demands a loyalty to

a transcendent church-community with a common faith and sacramental practice.[23]

Church membership, which both respects the individual and insists on the Church's transcendent goals, may be in tension with the goals of particular families.

Christian history has indicated a number of ways in which this conflict of values is manifest. Paul emphasized that blood relationship is subordinate to our kinship in Christian faith. Jesus himself asserted that it was not physical relationship to him that made one a disciple but doing the will of the Father. He asked his followers to leave their families behind even to the point of letting the dead bury the dead. One was to seek the Kingdom first; all family considerations were to be secondary. In the new order that Jesus proclaimed, neither blood relationship nor kinship was to count.

This family-Church tension has been continued in Christianity through the founding of religious orders which became new families, the institution of celibacy which gave up family life for the sake of the Kingdom, and the establishment of the principle of the equality of all before God, who is no respecter of persons. What we see here is the conflicting claims of two groups with different values and priorities. But this is to miss the basic revolutionary thrust of Jesus' message in the context of a Jewish religion which put great emphasis on family membership. In this tension the Christian religion says that the family is important but that it is not all-important, for there are more fundamental values that cannot be achieved merely through family membership. In fact there may be values that can be achieved only if family values are transcended or even rejected.

This tension between family values and Gospel values

has not always been recognized. When this tension is not recognized there is a real danger of domesticating religious values—of removing religious concerns from the broader community and restricting them to family concerns. A religious and a moral education that does not recognize this tension can end up being merely an education concerned with socializing the young and validating the family at the expense of broader values. Callahan sees a particular value in maintaining this family-Church tension in the area of moral education when she contends that

> Christianity breaks open the family, especially the extended family, and sees it as secondary to the Kingdom. The family is a means, not an end. The Christian family must be focused outside itself to an ultimate trans-ultimate future. Within the family the individual's conscience and integrity is ultimately valuable so that internal conflict may be inevitable. Tension and conflicts of value and interest must always exist when you affirm the value of a mediating, absolutely necessary institution of process, yet grant ultimate absolute value elsewhere.[24]

Persons involved in family ministry, especially as it relates to issues of moral development, must bear in mind this tension between family and Gospel values. Keeping this tension in mind will foster a broader view of family ministry. That such an approach to family ministry is necessary in this culture is supported by the Carnegie Study on Children. The study started out to study children within families but ended up as a lengthy analysis of social, economic, and political forces that impinge on children in families. The authors state:

We did not expect, at the start, to find ourselves considering at such length the economic and social forces that affect children and their parents. But we have learned from our work that much of the effort to help individuals . . . now seems unlikely to have a major social effect unless we also face and change the forces that make those individuals what they are and keep them that way.[25]

What I have written in this concluding section is not intended to minimize the importance of family ministry in the Church today and the importance of the family in the moral development of children. It is rather to propose a broadened moral education and family ministry that sees the role of the family realistically within the total cultural context. Family ministry should exist in the context of a church that works with families, youth, adults, intergenerational groupings, religious and public schools, social agencies, and the total community. Such a vision of family ministry demands a degree of cooperation that has not yet been found among church groups and community groups. The urgency of the situation makes such cooperation imperative.

Notes

1.   Charles H. Cooley, *Social Organization: A Study of the Larger Mind* (New York: Shocken, 1962), p. 23. First published 1909.
2.   Herbert J. Gans, *The Urban Villagers: Group and Class in the Life of Italian-Americans* (New

York: Free Press, 1962), chapter 5.

3. David Baumrind, "Child Care Practices Anteceding Three Patterns of Preschool Behavior," *Genetic Psychology Monographs* 75 (1967):43-88; "Current Patterns of Parental Authority," *Developmental Psychology* 4 (1971):1-13.

4. Andrew Greeley and Peter H. Rossi, *The Education of American Catholics* (Chicago: Aldine, 1966); Andrew Greeley, William C. McCready, and Kathleen McCourt, *Catholic Schools in a Declining Church* (Kansas City: Sheed & Ward, 1976); Christopher Jencks et al., *Inequality: A Reassessment of the Effect of Family and Schooling in America* (New York: Harper & Row, 1972).

5. Emile Durkheim, *Moral Education: A Study in the Theory and Application of the Sociology of Education* (New York: Free Press, 1973), p. 74. First published 1925.

6. Urie Bronfenbrenner, "The Role of Age, Sex, Class and Culture in Studies of Moral Development," *Religious Education* 47 (1952):3-17 (Research Supplement); Bronfenbrenner, and E. C. Devereau, "Patterns of Parent Behavior in America and West Germany: A Cross National Comparison," *International Social Science Journal* 14 (1962):488-506.

7. James S. Coleman et al., *Youth: Transition to Adulthood* (Chicago: University of Chicago Press, 1974), pp. 116-17.

8. H. Kent Geiger, *The Family in Soviet Russia* (Cambridge, Mass.: Harvard University Press, 1968), p. 89.

9. Middlesex, England: Penguin Books, 1971.
10. B. F. Skinner, *Beyond Freedom and Dignity* (New York: Knopf, 1971), chapter 4.
11. Martin Hoffman, "Development of Internal Moral Standards in Children," M. Strommen, ed., *Research on Religious Development* (New York: Hawthorn, 1971), p. 217.
12. *Obedience to Authority: An Experimental View* (New York: Harper & Row, 1974).
13. *Summerhill: A Radical Approach to Child Rearing* (New York: Hart, 1960).
14. "Moral Education" in Nancy and Theodore Sizer, *Moral Education: Five Lectures* (Cambridge, Mass.: Harvard University Press, 1970), p. 87.
15. *Social Learning Theory* (Englewood Cliffs, New Jersey: Prentice Hall, 1977), p. 22.
16. "Development."
17. Jean Piaget, *The Moral Judgment of the Child* (New York: Harcourt Brace & World, 1932).
18. Lawrence Kohlberg, "Stages of Moral Development as a Basis for Moral Education," in C.M. Beck et al., *Moral Education: Interdisciplinary Approaches* (New York: Paulist Press, 1971), pp. 23-92.
19. *Stage Theories of Cognitive and Moral Development: Criticisms and Application* (Cambridge, Mass.: Harvard University Press, 1976).
20. Lawrence Kohlberg, "Moral Development from the Standpoint of General Psychological Theory," in Thomas Lickona, ed., *Moral Development and Behavior: Theory, Research, and Social Issues* (New York: Holt, Rinehart & Winston, 1976), p. 50.

21. Gordon Allport, *The Individual and His Religion* (New York: Macmillan, 1950), chapter 3.
22. Carl Rogers, *Freedom to Learn* (Columbus, Ohio: Merrill, 1969), pp. 241-43.
23. Sidney Callahan, *Family Religious Education* (Washington, D.C.: National Conference of Diocesan Directors of Religious Education, 1974), p. 5.
24. Ibid., p. 20.
25. Kenneth Kenniston and the Carnegie Council on Children, *All Our Children: The American Family Under Pressure* (New York: Harcourt, Brace, Jovanovich, 1977), p. xv.

The Original Vision:
Children and Religious Experience

by Maria Harris

Maria Harris is well known for her work in parish religious education. The author of the D.R.E. Book, she has written widely on the topic of ministry and its relation to education, and has worked with religious educators throughout the country.

In this essay Maria Harris offers four guidelines for informing children's imagining of the divine. She then describes those qualities of family environment that best nurture the growth of religious experience in children.

Childhood cannot be fully understood simply by the observation of children. Quite apart from the difficulties of communication in the pre-adolescent years, there is often a dimension to our early experiences that we can only become fully conscious of in later life . . . in childhood, we may be wiser than we know.[1]

This passage from Edward Robinson's *The Original Vision* highlights several of the aspects of childhood I will pursue in this article. I will begin by pointing out the incompleteness of observational studies, especially in relation to the religious experience of children. Next, I will name some of the qualities of religious imagery and understanding appropriate to childhood and will point out that although naming these qualities is not always possible for children, religious experience is very much present. Finally, I will suggest four characteristics of a family environment which can nurture and extend the innate wisdom of childhood as it grows toward the more fully realized experience of a religious adulthood.

Beyond Observation

Religious education in our time is in debt to the rich insights continually being gained from developmental studies, whether these are of cognitive, moral, psychological, or faith development. Piaget's observation of young children, Erikson's reports of his own clinical work, Kohlberg's ongoing research, and the still-valuable works of Ronald Goldman have helped educators toward an understanding of how inner structures develop from infancy toward maturity. The contributions of most of these researchers are invaluable, and I have no wish to deny them. However, I do want to shift the focus in these pages from what we know through observational study toward those aspects of child life which are less measurable or observable but are nevertheless quite real in the child's experience. Sometimes observational and developmental studies allow portions of life which of their nature cannot be measured to slip away from attention, as water slips through the finest net.

My first concern here is with the child's early experiences of the divine.

Researchers at the Religious Experience Research Unit of Manchester College, Oxford, have been collecting accounts by adults of such remembered experiences, and what is significant about many of them is that although they occurred in the earliest years, they were recollected and describable only decades later. The most striking accounts, many of which are published in *The Original Vision,* came as responses to an appeal made by Sir Alister Hardy, founder of the Research Unit. In newspapers and magazines throughout Britain, he invited all those who "felt that their lives had in any way been affected by some power beyond themselves" to write an account of the experience and the effect it had had on their lives. No mention was made of childhood; nonetheless, some 15% of those responding (respondents now number well over 4000) started by going back to events and experiences of their earliest years.[2] Several examples follow.

> As a small child one of my favorite festivals was Trinity Sunday. It seemed to me quiet and beautiful, and happening around midsummer became associated in my mind with green trees and flowers in bloom. It was 'mysterious' and right, something far bigger than the words used

in church about it which sounded to a small child
nonsense. But Trinity wasn't nonsense, it was
Holy, holy, holy, as we sang in the hymn, and
even a very young child could join in a sort of
'oneness' with all things bright and beautiful and
worship this Something so great and lovely that it
didn't matter at all that it was not understood. It
just WAS. (Female, 64).[3]

• • • •

Neither my mother nor father attempted to explain or describe God to me. He was in-
describable as far as I was concerned, a Creator.
But I am sure my parents increased my sense of
God's omnipotence and mystery by their own
awe and reserve in discussing the subject.
(Female, 23).[4]

• • •

My mother was an atheist, my father an agnostic.
I suppose we heard of Christianity when we went
to school. Religious ideas came through books,
the coloured fairy books, myths, legends of
Greece and Rome, Tales of Norsemen, etc.
Religious feelings came from beautiful surround-
ings, the cycle of seasons, animal life-cycles, looking at a speck of dust on a pond, and reflecting
that inside oneself there was a centre of quietness
to be built up like this in expanding concentric
circles. (Female, 35).[5]

• • •

My early religious ideas, i.e. in terms of formal concepts, of God, angels and so on, were derived from family, church and school. However, though I repeated these concepts automatically, a kind of good manners like saying Thank You and Please, I distinctly recall regarding such concepts as no more than conventions, which it was politic to subscribe to in order to be thought of as a nice child, or a good child. *Real* religious experience at that time lay in incidents of the Browning "Sunset Touch" variety, i.e. feelings of significance. I don't mean simply that I was significant, but that *all* of which I was a part was meaningful. (Male, 44).[6]

.   .   .

To my mind, these accounts reveal several pressing questions and concerns fundamental to the religious education of children. First is the *breadth* of imagery for the Holy, the sacred, the divine, which individual persons employed. They speak of "green trees and flowers in bloom," "Something great and lovely," "animal life-cycles," "a centre of quietness," "Sunset Touch." But the issue is even more complex than individual images. Ana-Maria Rizzuto writes that God, for example, is not the creation of the child alone, but most times is offered by the parents to the child: God is presented as invisible but nonetheless real. In addition, children are often introduced to the "house of God," a place where God supposedly "dwells."[7] But at the same time, she continues, children bring their own God, the one they themselves have put together, to such conversations and encounters. They have met holiness in other places and have found God there as well. At such points, the God of "religion" and the God of the child face each other. "Reshaping, rethinking, and endless rumination, fantasies and defensive maneuvers, will come to help the child in his (or her) difficult task. This may decide the conscious religious future of the child. [It] is the critical moment for those interested in catechesis."[8] How are parents and families to rise to the challenges that such critically important moments pose? How marry the images in the tradition with the images experienced by the young person without doing violence to either?

A related issue is that religious experience, if we can believe the *Original Vision* accounts (and no reason exists for disbelief), may occur very early in life but is often neither expressed nor expressible. Moreover, this experience seems to be of two kinds: It is an experience of the *numinous*, where the child has a primary awareness of the Holy, and it is an experience of the *mystical*, where the child seems to have an intuitive awareness that all things are one. ("Even a very young child could join in a sort of 'oneness' with all things"; "It didn't matter at all that it was not understood. It just WAS." "My sense of God's omnipotence and mystery . . ."; "I don't mean simply that I was significant, but that all of which I was a part was meaningful.") These accounts lead me to the focal questions of this essay. 1) What guides can help in the development of religious understanding, specifically of a sense of God and the Image of God; and 2) What environments can the family design to nurture and engender such realizations? In the next sections I will address these questions. The first section will be concerned with religious images, the second with family environments.

Religious Images

"God is not the creation of the child alone, but most times is offered by the parents to the child." A profound sense of the awesomeness and responsibility connected with presenting God's image to children might well be the best disposition to bring to this task. Indeed, the awe might prevent speaking at all were the task less important. Are there guides for parents as they attempt to speak of the holy to the unformed but nevertheless extraordinary imaginations of their children?

1. A first guideline is that the images presented be *appropriate to* the divine, and *appropriable by* the child. Thus, the words we apply to God ought to convey a hesitancy, a tentativeness, and a sense of the impossibility of ever completely naming the Name. Indeed, this is one of the first revelations we have of God. When Moses asked what the name was, the response was at best enigmatic: "I am who I am; I will be who I will be." The point I am making is that *appropriate to* any images for the divine we might choose is the accompanying sense and suggestion that the image is at best an approximation. With this awareness, we can proceed to share the received tradition: that God is Father, as Jesus taught us; that God is Creator, by whom all things are made; that God is Spirit, to be worshiped in spirit and in truth; that God is Love, and that those who abide in love abide in God, and God in them. But there are other possibilities for naming as well: images such as those in the *Veni Sancte Spiritus*, the Sequence for Pentecost, where the Holy One is invoked as "Rest in labor," "Cool respite in heat," "Comfort in weeping." Such images, going beyond the personal, remind us that *person* itself is a

metaphor, an image. It may even be appropriate to compare God to non-human nature. Mark Van Doren, who taught Thomas Merton at Columbia, wrote of his brother in this simple poem:

CARL

Like a great tree
Spread over me
With love in every limb:
I worshipped him.[9]

It seems to me appropriate (or at least not inappropriate) to speak to God in some such fashion: God *might* be *like* "a great tree, spread over me with love in every limb."

At the same time, however (and here I am on speculative ground), it seems to me that the images for the Divine presented to the child need to be *appropriable by* the child. Here I might raise a quiet Christian question: How does the continued and exclusive use of the pronouns *he, his,* and *him* to refer to the Deity affect young children's perception of God? As young adults, will they come to reject God because of this usage? Is this masculine image capable of appropriation by persons—male and female—with a feminist consciousness? *Do* the pronouns convey that God is male, or is it possible to separate the words from the reality? What might all of these questions suggest for a developing prayer life in the young child? Similarly, what is the power of the exclusive use of parental images for God (Father *and* Mother) in the formation of the God-representation?[10]

The extraordinarily personal nature of much religious

experience underlines the importance of such questions. "My enquiries indicate that the commonest situation in which people report numinous or mystical experience is when they are alone or in silence, and they feel it belongs to the most private and secret core of their existence," writes David Hay.[11] Perhaps we need to explore those images which are common to both human and non-human nature, as Thomas Clarke has done in his probing of the meaning of the Center. Commenting on the traditional symbol of God as the sphere whose center is everywhere and whose circumference is nowhere, Clarke writes:

> When, as a modern Christian, I yield to the attraction of journeying to the center of my being, my faith tells me that this center is both my own human self, the image of God that I am, and the Self of God. . . . Without a pantheistic identifying of Creator and creature, without denying that the self-gift of God is totally gift, grace, I as a Christian affirm (and as a praying Christian I act on the affirmation of) this unfathomable mystery of the Holy Spirit dwelling within my spirit, as the divine Self selfing my human self: and hence as transforming Center of my center.[12]

2. The communal is a second guide assisting children toward religious experience/understanding. Communal images are of at least three kinds. Children (and adults) need to understand that in praying they use not only internal, mental images but their bodies as well. Thus the first "communal" relationship is that of one's inner word or thought and its outward, bodily expression. The Shaker hymn "It's a Gift to Be Simple" captures this in the words "When true simplicity is gained, to *bow* and to *bend* we

will not be ashamed."[13] Bowing, bending, walking in procession, making the sign of the cross, genuflecting, kneeling, kissing, joining hands in prayer, and even lying prostrate are signs of the body's outward expression of spiritual movement. These actions are found in the religious cultures of all peoples. Especially for children, whose conceptual powers are generally not developed, such community with their own bodies is a valuable and even necessary accompaniment to their sacred journey.

The communal is also expressed in the child's relationship to the non-human universe. Caryll Houselander once wrote that it is not foreign to a child to realize that clouds are God's thoughts. Psalm 19 reminds us, "The heavens are telling the glory of God. . . . Day to day pours forth speech, and night to night declares knowledge." Annie Dillard writes of waking in the arms of a god who is the day.[14] All of these—clouds, heavens, night, day—are sources prodding the child's (shall I say "natural"?) awareness of her or his companionship with the rest of creation. Perhaps this is most vivid in the child's relationship to food and drink, especially the often-denigrated "playing" with food. We have lost some of the sense captured in the word *companionship*, which has its etymology in the Latin *cum* and *panis*, "with bread." One does not eat and drink voraciously and care-less-ly when one realizes kinship with food born from common createdness, a kinship affirmed by the custom of Grace at meals. Perhaps it is not too farfetched to suggest a tie between the abuse of food that results from an ethos of domination and an absence of reverence, and a hungry world desperate for bread.

The most obvious communal element in a child's religious experience, however, is the community and companionship of other human beings. Religious

understanding and spiritual vision can become narcissistic
if completely individual. A growing sense of the Divine that
excludes all but God and self is an aborted and stunted
sense. To flourish as religious beings, children need to grow
toward a common sisterhood/brotherhood with all persons—with humanity everywhere. They can be helped to
this by seeing adults praying together; by experiencing
themselves as part of praying communities, both at home
and at worship in church or synagogue; by learning to lean
on the prayer of others through asking for and giving family
blessings in the evening (a custom sadly unused in our
time); by reviving the custom of asking for the prayers of
others; and by being taught prayer for those beyond
themselves—often in greater need than they are—as an integral element of religious life. Robinson shares an account
of one such powerful, offbeat, but deeply remembered
communal experience:

> My first real apprehension of religion that I can
> recall came from the housemaid, Alice, who was
> an enthusiastic follower of the Salvation Army.
> She would teach us choruses which we sang all
> together—"Pull for the Shore, Sailor" . . . and it
> was with her one evening that I first got an idea of
> the immense and lonely blackness of the night,
> and the distance of the stars, hence a sense of the
> power and strangeness of God, for I don't think I
> ever questioned His existence. (Male, 39).[15]

Elise Boulding shares another:

> As a child I was told that grandfather spent an
> hour every morning and evening listening to

God. So when I came suddenly upon my grandfather one day seated motionless in his armchair with closed eyes I knew he was not asleep. He was talking with God. I stopped short where I was and stood very still. Perhaps if I listened intently enough I might hear God's voice speaking to my grandfather. But the room remained quiet, not even the faintest whisper reached my ears. After a long time my grandfather opened his eyes, saw me, and smiled at me gently. These moments of intense listening for God's voice in the room with my grandfather are among the most vivid memories of my early childhood.[16]

Mystical and numinous experience culminates for many children in the integration of their own bodiliness, the non-human, and other people. *With, in, over* and *through* each and all of these, they come to sense a communion *not* like any of those just mentioned, yet inclusive of *all*. This is a Communion with the Holy Itself—a Communion that is not one more in a series of communal relations, but the Ground and Depth and Being of all existing Communion. Whitehead speaks of religion as "the transition from God the Void to God the Enemy, and from God the Enemy to God the Companion."[17] The experience of children, however, often *begins* with the sense of God as Companion.

I remember my first consciousness of God as a loving presence when, as quite a small child, I found myself alone in a wood; it was still and peaceful, and God was there and that was enough. (Female, 61).[18]

Since my very early childhood, 4 or 5, I had the
feeling of a Presence. This Presence was of great
comfort always, especially as I suffered from
asthma and the feeling of this Presence always
had a very good effect. (Female, 47).[19]

Indeed, this "sense of Presence" goes even
deeper—from the sense of a Presence with, to a Presence
with-in. Adults would be wise, in their religious meetings
with children, to speak the words of Psalm 139 (old 138)
and to recall the core of the eighth chapter of Romans. Both
are testimonies to the ancient religious belief that the Spirit
of God is within us, giving us words and shaping our
solitude, from the time of formation in our mother's womb.
Such an indwelling is one that children often know instinc-
tively but cannot name. It is their assurance that they need
never be alone.

3. Although this is perhaps controversial in a way those
mentioned thus far are not, I would argue for a third guide
as essential to genuine religious understanding: awareness
of the *political* and *societal*. Gregory Baum has written that
one's ethos and milieu shape one's religious vision.[20] It is
possible, however, that a child, especially a child of the
relatively affluent majority in the United States, may be so
cushioned from the realities of poverty, hunger, and need
in the rest of the world that he or she never grows toward a
prophetic religious vision or toward one which at least includes the prophetic. In contrast, there is a substantial
minority of children in this country, and a majority
throughout the rest of the world, who know firsthand
about being poor.

It is witnessing the agony on your mother's face as
she places hot cloths on your belly to quiet the

hunger pains.

It is never attending one school for more than a few months, and never having books and warm clothes.

It is selling a dozen eggs needed by the family because you cannot bear the shame of not bringing your share of soft drinks for the school picnic.[21]

For children who are born into, and grow through life in, such dread-full human need, religion may be drug or opiate, but in a world such as ours, this is unlikely. For such children, and for their more fortunate contemporaries who eventually do develop a global perspective, I suggest that the only image of God which can hold meaning is of a Divinity who proclaims release to the captives, sight to the blind, hearing to the deaf, food to the hungry, and hope to the despairing. No religious vision is complete without such an image.

4. A final guide for shaping a child's religious awareness is a sense of the Comic element in the Holy. I do not intend blasphemy here. Instead, I direct attention to the comic as "a narrow escape." Christopher Fry calls the comic an escape, "not from truth, but from despair; a narrow escape into faith."[22] Fry believed that there is an angle of experience where the dark is distilled into light, either in this life or another one, either in or out of time. It is this angle of experience I mean in speaking of the comic and in relating it to the religious experience of childhood. Children are often able to keep open comic possibility in the midst of tragedy; buoyancy in the face of shipwreck; hope for a happy ending despite warnings of disaster. They also

have a capacity for that peculiar kind of knowing that holds opposites together at the same time and does not insist absolutely on evidence for every phenomenon. Only if one is completely biased does one insist that this knowing is inferior to adult cognition. Although it is often different, unsystematic, and disorganized, it is neither inadequate nor weak nor wrong-headed—unless one is prejudiced to only one's own (often "grownup") point of view.

I suspect most children could agree with John Dominic Crossan that *if* one has been taught or has taken for granted that reality shows some overarching pattern of meaning and then comes to doubt the existence of such a plan, it is easy to claim that the world is meaningless and absurd.[23] However, most children are aware, with Crossan, that another reading of the situation would be that the world simply *is:* comic, yes; ambiguous, yes; paradoxical, yes; puzzling, certainly. But not necessarily absurd. (The children could not of course *say* this, but they would *know* it.) The absence of an obvious master plan simply means that in all circumstances the creature must allow the Divinity, the Holy, the Sacred, to be Itself. "I am who I am; I will be who I will be." To make this point, Crossan writes:

> Consider four assertions. First, the Holy has a great and secret master plan for the universe in process of gradual but inevitable realization. Second, this overarching scheme is known only to chosen initiates. Third, alternatively, the cosmic plan is a mystery and thus inscrutable to all human intellect. Fourth, the Holy has no such plan at all and that is what is absolutely incomprehensible to our structuring, planning, ordering minds.[24]

Such recognition of the comic preserves the autonomy of the Divine. If the goal of religion is adoration, perhaps the comic, more than the tragic, provides the possibility of genuine prayer: Where the structural security of one's human world is shattered, the Divine is able to touch the human heart, and merely human consciousness is brought to final genuflection.[25] Not being able to speak adequately of the Divine is a characteristic of childhood. Recognizing this allows adults to realize that neither full consciousness nor full articulation is necessary to religious experience, and that incomplete consciousness and the absence of communication are often signs that in childhood "we may be wiser than we know."

A Design for Family Environments

Which qualities can best nurture the growth of religious experience in children? Although the desired qualities are not exclusive to the family, they are found there in ideal form. Recently, their importance has tended to be eclipsed. In large part, the eclipse is a result of twentieth-century United States' passion for bureaucracy and its characteristic qualities: division of labor, secrecy, credentialing, qualification, objectivity (in the sense that rules and regulations come before persons), and precision (in the sense that technical skill is valued more than human affectivity). Families, however, are not bureaucratic organizations. They are communal forms meant especially for the rearing of the young and for helping new generations understand their own possibilities.[26] For developing specifically religious possibilities, a different set of characteristics is needed. I propose four: sacramentality, solitude, tolerance of failure, and commencement.

Sacramentality. I use the word *sacramentality* in two ways. In its first meaning it affirms that bodily, material, physical reality can be the place where the divine and the human meet. In practice in family life, this would mean that family attitudes to bodiliness shape attitudes to the spiritual, if by the latter one means "matter and more." Touching or not touching; sexuality as positive, or sex as evil; the presence or absence of art and athletics; the relationship to food—these make possible the kind of individual and communal entrance into prayer described above in discussing images.

The second meaning of sacramentality is both more and less obvious: the sacramental as central to the life of the Church, and the sacraments of the Church as vehicles for the divine. These aspects are the more obvious element; what may be less obvious is that although Baptism as religious ritual is experienced in the Church setting, the realities of birth, entrance into and acceptance by a community are faced and found in the family setting. Confirmation, as the approval, naming, and acceptance of vocation in life and direction toward adulthood as a Christian, is shaped in the family. Forgiveness as central to reconciliation is celebrated in the *ecclesia,* but to know its deepest meaning, one must meet such forgiveness in the *ecclesiola* which is the family unit. So too with the other sacraments: Communion with God is intimately tied to community and to communion with those closest to the child; final anointing is, ideally, a seal upon a life where blessing has first been understood in the healing touch of a parent, grandparent, brother, or sister.

Solitude. "Loneliness," writes May Sarton, "is the poverty of self; solitude is the richness of self."[27] Solitude is very difficult for the poor; it is a luxury of the wealthy and of the middle class. Nonetheless, an ideal to be striven for is that all children have pockets and spaces in their lives where they are free to enjoy solitude; to be by themselves; to take time for laziness, and to make the siesta (in whatever form) the center of their spiritual, religious lives.

Loneliness, isolation, and abandonment can be genuine terrors for a child, just as they are for adults. Genuine solitude, on the other hand, provides the opportunity for children to be "watchers," observing life, getting the feel of it, sensing its flow and its rhythm. The bombardment of noise from stereos and the drug-like quality of much television are certainly not conducive to solitude; more often they are its rivals or enemies. To counteract them, every home or apartment might have designated "quiet rooms" or "quiet spaces" where the family members are encouraged to explore the stillness and silence inside and outside themselves. Perhaps families could arrange for one hour a week, or one half-day a month, when they would agree to be quiet together to discover the riches in solitude.

Solitude is not necessarily limited, however, to the absence of sound. As privacy, it can take the form of an absence of probing, judging, interrupting, criticizing. Parents and siblings often know one another's sorest spots; one reminder of the perverse presence of original sin is the temptation in families to go for the jugular via teasing when one of the members—often the youngest—would much prefer being left alone. Allowing for the privacy of such aloneness is the beginning of a prayerful attitude and atmosphere conducive to contemplation. When families take seriously the suggestion to build upon this privacy, they contribute mightily to the possibility of religious experience.

Tolerance of failure. One of Robert Frost's most

memorable verses has to do with home. "Home is the place where, when you have to go there, they have to take you in."[28] So too with failure: Home is the place where it must be met; people live too closely in families, in the physical sense, to hide failure when it occurs. The family's attitude to failure—in school, in games, in sport, in love—has a great influence on children's power to distinguish between trying and not succeeding, and between sin and evil.

If it is true, as suggested above, that the comic is a narrow escape into faith, one of the times for making that escape to faith comes when the child experiences failing in others or in self. The loss of innocence may even need to happen *(O felix culpa!)* if the child is to come to a deeper understanding that the Presence referred to as the Presence of God is a Presence that remains even if the child is unworthy. In the Christian tradition, where death and resurrection are the kerygmatic center of the gospel message, acceptance of failure is essential to a grasp of the paschal mystery.

Families, especially the adult members, can make such acceptance a possibility for children if they themselves are able to accept failure. Often, the child is ready and able to do so, but because parents want to experience success through their children's lives rather than through their own, children are either not permitted to fail or are told that their pain, distress, anger, or misery is not real. Such courses of action can do great damage. The alternative is simpler: Allow the family to be a real world of real humans where many mistakes are made, where messiness and ambiguity are never far away, where lost tempers are admitted and found, and where failure is acknowledged and owned. In such settings, the seeds of forgiveness, redemption, resurrection, and transformation may be buried for awhile, but eventually they will flower from the hard and bitter ground.

Commencement. By referring to the family as a place of commencement I mean that it is a place that succeeds if its members can leave it. A family is a community that can let go. To understand how difficult this can be, one need only ask any parent what it is like to send a child out to the first day of school; to "give away" a child in marriage; to watch a child choose a different path from the one the parent thinks best. The pain in the situation is that raising children, when it is truly loving, is in the direction of a dependent independence. It is helping the young as they grow older to choose and to make their own decisions. It is enabling them to discover their own unique gifts and thus no longer to need yours the way they did as children.

Commencement is the act of starting on the journey that life itself is. To help children move in the exploratory way of such journeys, families can tell the stories of the great religious travelers: Abraham and Sarah; Naomi and Ruth; Paul; Jesus of Nazareth. Families can also be places characterized by exploration, places where new things are tried. They can be the setting for brief initial journeys, for short forays, before the larger, longer adult journey claims its time. But when that moment comes, the way in which the family is the place of commencement lies in its style of letting go.

Another way of describing growing up is to say it is the time a person knows that it is all right to leave. A strength is given in such a time for the young person to say of her or his family. "These people trust me. They aren't saying a lot, they aren't giving me orders, but they hear me, they care, and they believe in my own eternal beginning of the journey to which I'm called. They think I can do it." The poetic irony in the situation is well known: Once the vision beyond the family, the going out, the exodus, is allowed, it is possible to come back; indeed, it is the only way to assure return. The end of all exploring is arriving at the place from which we started and knowing it for the first time. If, from the beginning, the environment has been one that indicated "God is where you are going," the irony will not change. If the family environment has been sacramental, has allowed for solitude, and has tolerated failure, then wherever the journey takes the child, now grown, it will be in the direction of Home. And Home, let us hope, will be a realization of the Original Vision of Holiness, Wisdom, and Wonder.

Notes

1. Edward Robinson, *The Original Vision* (Oxford: Religious Experience Research Unit, 1977), p. 8.
2. Ibid., p. 11.
3. Ibid., p. 28.
4. Ibid., pp. 65-66.
5. Ibid., p. 71.
6. Ibid., p. 68.
7. Ana-Maria Rizzuto, M.D., *The Birth of the Living God* (Chicago: University of Chicago Press, 1979), p. 8.
8. Ibid.
9. See *Morning Worship and Other Poems* (New York: Harcourt, Brace & Company, 1959), p. 86.
10. Rizzuto's *The Birth of the Living God* is one of the few analytic studies of the formation of the image of God in children. The author appears to

assume that the image of God is tied to children's parental images, although she leaves open other possibilities. See n. 7 above.

11. In "Religious Experience and Education," *Learning for Living* 16, 3 (Spring 1977):160.

12. In Thomas Keating et al., *Finding Grace at the Center* (Still River, Mass.: St. Bede Publications, 1978), pp. 52-53.

13. Carla de Sola, in *Learning Through Dance* (New York: Paulist Press, 1974), describes how the dance may be danced and sung with the gracious accompaniment of movement. See pp. 174-75.

14. In *Holy the Firm* (New York: Harper & Row, 1977), p. 11, Dillard writes, "Every day is a god, each day is a god, and holiness holds forth in time."

15. Robinson, *The Original Vision*, p. 67.

16. Boulding shares this quote from Helen Thomas Flexner's *Quaker Childhood* in her brief pamphlet, *Children and Solitude* (Wallingford, Pa.: Pendle Hill, 1962), pp. 20-21.

17. See Alfred North Whitehead, *Religion in the Making* (New York: World Publishing Company, 1960), p. 17.

18. Quoted in Timothy Beardsworth, *A Sense of Presence* (Oxford: Religious Experience Research Unit, 1977), p. 120.

19. Ibid.

20. In *The Social Imperative* (New York: Paulist Press, 1979), p. 129. See especially his essay "Spirituality and Society," pp. 129-47. See also his essay "Prayer and Society," in Gloria Durka and Joanmarie Smith, eds., *Emerging Issues in Religious*

Education (New York: Paulist Press, 1976), pp. 18-28.

21. Arthur Jones, "Poverty: 'The Scars Never Heal'" in *National Catholic Reporter*, June 15, 1979, p. 14.

22. John Dominic Crossan, *Raid on the Articulate* (New York: Harper & Row, 1976), quotes Fry on p. 17.

23. Ibid. See especially "First Variation: Comedy and Transcendence," pp. 9-54.

24. Ibid., p. 44.

25. Ibid., p. 123.

26. See Gabriel Moran, "The Way We Are: Communal Forms and Church Response," in Maria Harris, ed., *Parish Religious Education* (New York: Paulist Press, 1978), pp. 25-40.

27. In *Mrs. Stevens Hears the Mermaids Singing* (New York: W.W. Norton, 1965), p. 183.

28. The line is from "The Death of the Hired Man," in *North of Boston* (New York: Henry Holt, 1914), p. 20.

For Further Reading

Baum, Gregory. "Spirituality and Society." *Religious Education* 72 (May-June 1978):266-83.

Boulding, Elise. *Children and Solitude.* Wallingford, Pennsylvania: Pendle Hill, 1962.

Crossan, John Dominic. *Raid on the Articulate.* New York: Harper & Row, 1976.

Dillard, Annie. *Holy the Firm.* New York: Harper & Row, 1977.

_____. *Pilgrim at Tinker Creek*. New York: Harper & Row, 1974.

Harris, Maria. "Prayer and Vision." *P.A.C.E.* 10. Winona, Minn.: St. Mary's Press, 1979.

Keating, Thomas, et al. *Finding Grace at the Center*. Still River: St. Bede, Mass.: 1979.

Rizzuto, Ana-Maria. *The Birth of the Living God*. Chicago: University of Chicago Press, 1979.

Robinson, Edward. *The Original Vision*. Manchester College, Oxford: Religious Experience Research Unit, 1977.

A Neglected Ministry: Special-Needs Children and Their Families

by Gloria Durka

Gloria Durka directs the Division of Children's Education and Family Ministry in the Graduate School of Religion and Religious Education at Fordham University. She has co-authored Modeling God *and co-edited* Emerging Issues in Religious Education *and* Aesthetic Dimensions of Religious Education.

In this essay she attempts to broaden the reader's understanding of special-needs children and to indicate what ministry to families of such children would entail.

Most people would agree that children with special needs, and their families, have a right to be full members of their parish communities. Yet the recent National Catechetical Inventory has shown that little effort has been made to make such full participation a reality.[1]

The survey reveals that only 43% of reporting parishes provide catechetical assistance for the "handicapped," 42% for children with learning disabilities, 27% for the emotionally disturbed or socially maladjusted, and 14% each for blind or partially seeing and deaf or hard of hearing. Almost 50% of the responding DREs reported that preschool children who have special needs have no programs in their parish that can assist them, and 33% reported that young and middle-aged special-needs adults also have no such programs. This sad state of affairs looks even worse when combined with the broader picture. For example, most parishes do not provide liturgies or special aids to those with special needs, and more than 50% have not taken into consideration physical barriers which make accessibility to buildings difficult or even impossible.

In this essay I will attempt to demonstrate that there are more special-needs children in United States society (and in our parishes) than is commonly assumed, that differences in need must be recognized, tested, and questioned, and that religious educators and family ministers must respond to these different needs with suitable programs and materials. I will suggest that we must minister to special-needs children within the family context, and I will conclude by suggesting some concrete ways of implementing this ministry at the parish level.

Why Use the Term "Special Needs"?

What do we mean by special-needs children, and why should we use this descriptive term instead of the now-common expressions such as *handicapped, disabled,* or *retarded?*

Labels such as *handicapped, disabled,* or *retarded* stigmatize children and often have other bad results. Yet our faith in labels and definitions and our reliance on them is debatable at best: The human condition is too complex to be straitjacketed into a simple formulation. For example, *handicap* is a social concept, depending on how society defines it.

A key issue for educators and ministers is the *criterion* by which we separate, for instance, the "handicapped" from the "nonhandicapped," or the retarded from the nonretarded. Let us look at some examples from recent history. During the first half of this century and particularly following World War I, we placed ever-increasing reliance on intelligence tests as a presumably objective measure of ability. Intelligence was considered a global and static entity. This presumption gave the intelligence-test ratings a deceptive finality. Once retarded, always retarded—it was presumed that one dealt with an irreversible, unchanging condition.

In 1973, the American Association on Mental Deficiency published a revised manual which drastically reversed the 1959-1961 version by setting the upper limit of mental retardation at two standard deviations below the norm—that is, at an IQ of 68 on the Stanford-Binet Test.[2] Since the AAMD terminology is generally accepted in the United States as the appropriate standard-setter, publication of the 1973 manual revision miraculously restored millions of mentally retarded American citizens to normalcy. This demonstrates to what extent our criteria determine whether a child is to be considered "handicapped."

A similar situation exists with regard to the *testing procedures* by which criteria are applied. In retrospect it is not just embarrassing but quite amazing that it took action in the courts on behalf of children kept in mental retardation programs to establish that it was faulty to use an English-language test to determine the general intelligence level of children raised in non-English-speaking families, such as Mexican-American families in California.[3]

Again, research done on agency *classification procedures* for children—procedures based on standardized intelligence tests—reveals that such procedures resulted in labeling as mentally retarded a disproportionately large number of Chicanos and Blacks. Current classification procedures often violate the rights of children to be evaluated within a culturally appropriate normative framework, their right to be assessed as multi-dimensional beings, their right to be fully educated, their right to be free of stigmatizing labels, and their right to cultural identity and respect.

The bias which labeling promotes is not confined to limiting the potential intellectual and psychosocial development of children. Persons working in the field of *physical "handicap"* are tempted to think that in contrast to the vagaries of the concept of intelligence, they are dealing with objective physical factors that can be measured accurately. However, this view is increasingly challenged—for instance, in the field of visual and auditory impairments. Even the most persuasive "objective" criteria show upon closer scrutiny how much room they leave for subjective coloring on the part of the individual tester or of those prescribing test procedure and interpretation.[4]

Research has shown that in many instances testers and test prescribers are not able to separate their own cultural bias from the interpretation of test results. Thus, for example, children who are presumed to come from families of low socioeconomic status are often "expected" to perform less adequately than middle-class children with a similar physical impairment. In such cases the diagnosis and the treatment are often inadequate or inappropriate.

When children are misdiagnosed this way, their overall physical growth and development can be delayed or seriously hindered, and their physical impairment can even worsen.

Even carefully chosen terminology can bring mixed results, as in our use of the expression *learning disabilities.* The United States Office of Education has identified children with special (specific) learning disabilities as those who exhibit a disorder in one or more of the basic *psychological* processes involved in understanding or using spoken or written language. These disabilities may be manifested in disorders of listening, thinking, talking, reading, writing, spelling, or arithmetic. They include conditions such as perceptual handicaps, brain injury, minimal brain dysfunction, dyslexia, developmental phasia, and so on. They do not include learning problems which are due primarily to visual, hearing, or motor handicaps, to mental retardation, emotional disturbance, or environmental disadvantage.[5]

When the term *learning disabilities* is used in the sense just described, it has had the beneficial effect of helping us identify disorders specifically, accurately. As a result, many children who had been listed as mentally retarded, emotionally disturbed, slow learners, or perceptually handicapped can now be precisely identified in terms of specific learning disabilities.

Yet some difficulty remains, since the term *learning disabilities* is sometimes used loosely as referring to any learning *problem.* The visually impaired, for example, do of course have learning *problems,*[6] and it is easy to slip into calling those problems learning *disabilities.*

Faulty labeling is even harder on a group of children whose exceptional needs cause their families, at whatever income level, extraordinary financial strain: those with *physical impairments.* For a child who is blind or deaf, confined to a wheelchair, or afflicted with cerebral palsy, the possibility of leading a normal childhood is gravely imperiled not only by the often-prohibitive cost of training, equipment, transportation, and counseling that it takes to give such a child simply an even chance, but by our society's deep-seated attitudes toward "handicapped" persons. Deeply ingrained in our day-to-day transactions is the tendency to single out those who are "different," to affix a label to them, and to relate to this label an expected performance which accentuates their difference and takes for granted that they will function inadequately. Thus a label can become a personal libel that produces social and economic consequences not always realized by the person who does the labeling.

Those who suffer from mental *retardation* are also the victims of poor labeling. About 6 million persons in the United States are considered to be mentally retarded; of these, about 2.5 million are under 20 years of age.

The retardation in one quarter of all those 6 million persons can be linked to genetic, infectious, and accidental causes for which there are as yet no effective preventive or curative measures. But three quarters can be traced to inadequacies in prenatal and perinatal health care, nutrition, and child-rearing and to a dearth of social and environmental opportunities. As the President's Panel on Mental Retardation observed in 1962,

> A number of experiments with the education of presumably retarded children from slum neighborhoods strongly suggests that a predominant cause of mental retardation may be lack of learning opportunities and absence of 'intellectual vitamins' under these adverse environmental conditions.[7]

Likewise it is important not to apply the term *retarded* to those children who may need some enrichment and reinforcement assistance but who are essentially normal, or to those who are educationally disadvantaged because they are ill housed, ill clad, or ill fed. Moreover, serious questions must be raised about extending the term *handicapped children* from its present admittedly uncertain usage to include all children who are labeled delinquent or socially maladjusted or who are socioeconomically deprived or disadvantaged because of cultural differences. Poverty can certainly create handicapping conditions, and handicapped children of poor families face very serious problems. But it is quite a different matter to label a child as handicapped simply *because* the family is poor.

It seems clear, then, that the term *special-needs* is much more appropriate than terms such as *mentally retarded, learning disabled,* or *physically handicapped* because it does not carry with it the pejorative baggage which had had devastating effects on the rights of many children and their families. Labels are shortcuts for the convenience of the labeler and of the agencies dealing with the children, but they are of no advantage to the children, who frequently resent and oppose those labels. We must challenge the notion that it is necessary to label children in order to gain them access to specific services.

All those who work in family ministry must avoid careless labeling of chldren. Even the preferable term *special-needs children* is not enough; ministers must be able to recognize and name various *kinds* of special needs that children have. Such careful distinctions will not only help the minister to render better service but will help both the children and their families to understand and accept and deal with those special needs.

An Ecological View of Ministry to Special-Needs Children

The family minister must deal with the special-needs child not as an isolated individual but as an interacting member of a group with many relationships. The family is of course the nucleus of those relationships, so any attempt to minister to the child's needs must be made in the context of the family. The family, after all, performs such utterly basic functions as nurturing the child physically, teaching and modeling the basic social roles, and transmitting the techniques and values and customs of the family's culture, including its language—in short, helping the child become a well integrated, mature person.

Despite its basic responsibilities and many opportunities for promoting children's growth, in practice the family sometimes does very little for its children. Parents who are themselves deprived intellectually, culturally, morally, or financially, for example, often fail to give their children the support they need to blossom.

Family ministers, like many other would-be helpers,

often feel that they have recognized and tackled these family shortcomings, and they are at a loss to explain why they have apparently failed to overcome them. Several reasons might be:

First, we are traditionally reluctant to intervene in people's private affairs. So when we do intervene, we do it too late and with too little.

Secondly, we have focused programs too much on children from economically and socially disadvantaged families. Singling out families in one socioeconomic class automatically creates a two-class system of ministry and unnecessarily labels and demeans the families who receive the services. (As was illustrated earlier, many of the problems of special-needs children are not limited to the poor and the disadvantaged but affect members of all socioeconomic classes.)

Thirdly, many programs are categorical rather than comprehensive. They address a specific need such as helping a child and his or her family learn sign language, but they often do not deal with the daily living problems that a family with a deaf child has to face. Mechanisms for linking such "skill" programs with each other are tenuous. While categorical programs (e.g., special classes for the blind, for the speech impaired) are essential, resources of many kinds, and knowledge represented in many disciplines, must be brought to bear on problems in a coordinated manner.

What we need, then, is an ecological view of ministry for special-needs children. This view would develop services encompassing the child as a member of larger units: the child within the family first of all, but also the child in school, the child in church, the child within a particular subculture of society. This ecological point of view requires a search for services which, instead of plucking children from the natural environment in which they have grown and to which they will return, would reach children in that environment. In such a view of ministry, children are not asked to change individually in an unchanged environment. Rather, the whole community is affected by, nourished, and graced by the presence of the special-needs children in its midst. The community is, in effect, ministered *to* by the children.

How to Begin Ministry to Special-Needs Children and Their Families

Any religious education program attentive to special-needs children must start with two premises:

1. that people have such obvious bodily needs as food, clothing, shelter, and medical care;

2. that they also need nourishment for their minds and spirits, including the need to be
   - wanted, valued, accepted, and given a sense of belonging;
   - attended to, cared for, and protected;
   - educated and guided toward social capability and moral responsibility;
   - given opportunities for life satisfaction through useful work and creativity.

What are some implications for action that stem from these basic physical and spiritual needs? And where do we begin?

Here are several modest suggestions to family ministers, parish coordinators, and directors of religious education programs:

1. Acknowledge that every parish has special-needs children. This alone will influence decision-making

policies on the types of programs to offer, curriculum materials to use, and personnel to solicit.

2. Find out which children have special needs, and identify the needs. While children with physical handicaps such as blindness or muscular dystrophy are easy to notice if they attend services in the church, much greater efforts must be made to identify those who do not participate in either religious services or educational programs. These efforts could include the following:

    a. Hold a meeting of parents of special-needs children. An announcement in the parish bulletin and from the pulpit can help, but nothing can match one-to-one communication via a personal telephone call or visit. A few leadership couples or families could form a contact network.

    b. Visit the local schools personally. Most school principals and personnel are willing to help and can do so without disseminating confidential information.

    c. At the first meeting, invite those in attendance to contact other parents who have special-needs children.

    d. Discuss with teachers and parents (and later with the children) which kinds of programs, scheduling, and physical facilities would help the children who will be attending religious education classes and church services.

3. Solicit volunteer help from parishioners who are engaged in social service agencies or schools as child-care workers, special-education teachers, counselors, and therapists. Parishioners who have professional preparation to work with special-needs children would make ideal

catechists for these children.

4. Ask for volunteer adults and older adolescents who can work with these professionals and gain some paraprofessional experience in dealing with the special-needs children. In turn, the DRE or "master" teachers in the religious education program can help the professionals learn religious education content and methodology.

5. Pool the resources of small parishes with those of neighboring parishes.

6. Whenever possible, "mainstream" children into regular religious education classes. However, there will be times when they ought to have special classes.

7. In the annual budget make specific allocations for programs for special-needs children and their families.

8. Every year, take a hard look at the physical plant in which classes, services, and parish functions are held to see what can be done to give special-needs parishioners easier access to the facilities.

9. Form self-help groups to provide mutual support and encouragement and to help parents recognize and affirm their own roles as the primary religious educators of their children.

10. Screen and select teachers very carefully, considering not only their professional preparation but, even more important, their patience, understanding, and perseverance. All children need a warm emotional climate within which to function, but this is especially so for the children with special needs.

What should be stressed is that special-needs children can learn, that they have a right to be participant members of our church communities, and that much more needs to be done.

Conclusion

In a simple world, parents were the only advocates children needed. But in today's complex society they and their parents need the help of powerful, well organized agencies as well. The Church should be in the forefront of those helping agencies, and it should be particularly concerned about special-needs children and their families. The Church must do more than merely affirm the personal rights of such people. It must do more, even, than developing and applying new methods of prevention, treatment, and education. Rather, it must develop new, imaginative programs that will reorder the whole inter-relationship between the special-needs children, their families, and society at large. What better place to begin educating the community to its responsibility to those with special needs than in the local parish? And what better vehicle than a concerned and supportive parish community?

Notes

1. *A National Inventory of Parish Catechetical Programs* (Washington, D.C.: USCC Publications Office, 1978), pp. 35-36.
2. Herbert Grossman, ed., *Manual on Terminology and Classification in Mental Retardation* (Washington, D.C.: American Association on Mental Deficiency, 1973).

3. Gunnar Dybwad, "What Should Be Our National Policy Toward Handicapped Children?" *Raising Children in Modern America: Problems and Prospective Solutions.* Nathan B. Talbot, ed. (Boston: Little, Brown & Co., 1976), pp. 441-42.
4. Ibid.
5. Quoted in Samuel A. Kirk, *Educating Exceptional Children*, 2nd ed. (Boston: Allyn & Bacon, 1970), p. 189.
6. James J. McCarthy and Joan F. McCarthy, *Learning Disabilities* (Boston: Allyn & Bacon, 1969), p. xxi.
7. Quoted in Nathan B. Talbot, *Raising Children in Modern America: What Parents and Society Should Be Doing for Their Children* (Boston: Little, Brown & Co., 1976), p. 149.

For Further Reading

Benson, Dennis, and Stewart, Stan J. *The Ministry of the Child*. Nashville: Abingdon, 1978.

Clarke, Louise. *Can't Read, Can't Write, Can't Talk Too Good Either*. Baltimore: Penguin Books, 1974.

Ferber, Andrew; Mendelsohn, Marilyn; and Napier, Augustus. *The Book of Family Therapy*. Boston: Houghton Mifflin, 1972.

The Professions and the Family: Healing the Split

by Gabriel Moran

Gabriel Moran, FSC, a leading theorist in the field of religious education, has long been interested in the notion of community and its relationship to family. The author of ten books, he has worked with religious educators in diverse settings. His most recent book is Education Toward Adulthood.

In this essay he describes the split between the family and the modern professions and suggests concrete ways in which the professions—including the Church's various ministries—can better serve the family.

Family literature often goes in one of two directions. The more common path is to begin by bemoaning the disintegration of the family. Statistics are cited less for proving the case than for illustrating what is assumed to be obviously true. A counter movement in family literature tries to marshal other statistics which would show that the family has not collapsed.[1]

If I have to take sides in this dispute my sympathies lie with the second position. My reasons are: 1) Every generation in this country since 1607 has been certain that the family has just collapsed. Perhaps it finally has, but history should make us cautious on the point. 2) Any statistics that I have ever seen on such topics as abortion, divorce, and child abuse are at least ambiguous. Without an historical perspective the statistics prove very little.

It is a fact, nonetheless, that the doomsayers are in the majority or in any case produce more writing. This fact itself demands some explanation from those of us who do not accept the assumption that the family has disintegrated. My own formulation of a response would be that we do have a crisis in our *perception* of the family. What that means most immediately is that family is a dominant image in our perception of the world. When the world does not fit the image, we either overextend the image of family, which leads to a confused image, or else we try to fix up the world to make it fit a familial image.

This "crisis of perception" has to some extent accompanied the entire American experiment. The earliest English settlers came here to set up "true families" and familial churches.[2] From the second generation onward it was rather clear that the search would be frustrated, but our language still reflects both a dominance of the family imagery and the absence of other individual and communal imagery. Religious groups often skillfully exploit this unrealized hope for true families and familial churches. Sun Myung Moon in this respect is an heir of seventeenth-century Puritanism in promising that the Unification Church is a "true family."

The crisis thus comes about from the combining of two things: 1) the unclear but deeply rooted feelings that the human race associates with the word *family;* 2) the extension of the image of family to almost every kind of organization in the culture. Anyone looking for a family in a sports team, a law firm, an apartment complex, or a parish is bound to be disappointed. But the disappointment can always be taken next door to where the true family may be. Jane Howard has written: "Call it a clan, call it a network, call it a tribe, call it a family. . . . You need one because you are human." But it makes all the difference in the world whether you are looking for a network, a clan, or a family. And Howard in fact names what she is looking for in the title of her book: *Families.*[3]

I have indicated that the crisis of perception is longstanding. Is there anything new? Is it worse today? Since perception is largely a question of awareness, then the crisis is indeed greater today. Our age is if anything an age of increased awareness through worldwide communication. That is not to say that we have greater or deeper understanding—just that one can hardly avoid hearing about divorce rates, child abuse, or welfare mothers.

The change in the position of the family is not completely reducible to subjective awareness. There have been important structural and contextual changes in the family. As I shall indicate below, I think the major changes occurred in the early nineteenth century. However, some of the effects of those changes are still being felt, and several additional factors have continued to change in the twentieth century.

Twin factors that have been affecting the family in complex ways are: 1) the lengthening of the expected life span; 2) the increasing control of the process of procreation. Thus, at the turn of this century a woman could expect to marry young, have a sizeable family in which she was mother, and die before the last child left home. For a girl born in the 1960s or 1970s the pattern will almost certainly be different. Even if she becomes the mother of a family she is likely to have a third of her life remainng after she has played the role of mother.

Our attempt to express all personal relationships in terms of family imagery is leading us to increased confusion in the twentieth century. None of us can now define our whole adult life in reference to the family. A fast-growing minority of adults do not live at all in a family unit, unless the word *family* is extended to cover all human relationships. Lacking the imagery to describe our lives, we can only record our experience as a disintegration of the family.

The past and present confusion on this point might seem harmless enough. But our passionate concern for the family, together with our perception of its decline, can easily lead to hasty and ill-defined attempts to save the family. All kinds of people want to help the family, and their good intentions should not be cynically dismissed. But I do think there is a danger of people acting from mixed-up, nostalgic feelings about what the ideal family should be. People often agitate passionately for those things which they sense are absent from their own lives. Also, we have so institutionalized this family help that many large bureaucracies have a vested interest in the assumption that the family is in terrible shape and needs outside salvation.

This point brings me to the second concern in this essay: the professions. A cluster of jobs that claim to be new professions have gathered around the family. These psychological and social works are sometimes called "the helping professions," a phrase that would appear to be a nervous redundancy. All professions are supposedly helpful to someone, but certain professions in the twentieth century have been conceived with the needy family particularly in view.

If our perception of the family is to be improved, then the relation between the family and the professional is part of what has to be clarified. Not much has been written on this important question. One of the few lengthy treatments is Christopher Lasch's *Haven in a Heartless World*.[4] In the judgment of many people besides myself, Lasch seems blinded in this book by anger and despair. He not only assumes the destruction of the family but he names the destroyer: the professions that claim to help. His thesis would seem to be extreme, and it leads to no practical conclusion.

I am interested in covering some of the same territory. I do not assume that the family has been destroyed, so I need not find the culprit. I assume that the family is here to stay. I also assume that social workers, psychologists, school teachers, and church ministers are going to continue to exist. My question is: How can people with professional competencies be of help, albeit limited help, to existing families? The answer to that simple question requires an historical awareness of how the professions and the family split in the nineteenth century; that split was part of the centuries-old process of modernization. Professionals can help the family only if they heal some of the modern split that affects the family and its context.

The Family

By the word *family* I refer to the basic biological unit which the human race has had at least since the beginning of civilization. The central meaning of family has always been located in the relation of parents and children. At all times, including the present, the word *family* can reach out to other kinship. There is almost unlimited variation in how many relatives the word might encompass and how many other terms for kinship are used. In short, some of the *context* of the family has drastically changed, but the *central and primary unit* has changed hardly at all over the millenia.

This distinction between the central and primary unit of the family and the context of the family is crucial. The main issue is not whether aunt, grandparent, and cousin are included in the concept of the family. Far more important is the political and economic context of the family. The family's biggest weakness today is that it is not at the center of political and economic power. Adding relatives to the family would do little good for the family if its real problem is the huge concentrations of power to which the family is peripheral.

In pre-modern Western society the family clearly occupied a central role; that is, power resided within the family and in imagery derived from the family. Economically, the family was at the center of production. The clothing and the food that were needed originated from the family household. Economic cooperation cut across family lines, but the organization was visible and manageable from the family. The picture is not meant to be romantic: Many families lived in dire poverty, there was great inequality within rich families, and children had little time to grow up before they were thrown into the struggle for survival.

Politically, the family also held center stage. Even under monarchy the family influence is obvious. The king was a kind of super father. The citizens, especially the poor ones, were like children. They could be kept under control by the king and could be subjected to intrusions of privacy if suspected of not properly appreciating their protective custody.

The process called modernization was in large part the gradual change in this political and economic organization. With the right resources, some peoples began to reform the political and economic orders. Economically, the long process of industrialization shifted production away from the home to the factory. The answer to poverty and slavery appeared to be the introduction of machinery and the large-scale organizing of resources. Politically, the father was rebelled against and constitutional guarantees were sought. Even the kindliest of father kings was suspect unless there were other forms of political assembly and protection of rights. The family moved toward the periphery of economic power and political imagery.

The United States of America, it should be noted, was founded in the midst of this process. It was heir to the great Calvinist stress on family but was also subject to the loss of familial power in politics and economics. The Declaration of Independence was proclaimed in the same year that Adam Smith's *Wealth of Nations* appeared. Smith's description of natural resources, assembly-line production, and the free play of the marketplace found special expression in the United States. This nation became known for its love of technology and its inventive genius.

The family was not the productive unit in this new economic order. Poor families were for a while subjected to exploitation as family units. The Slater system in the Rhode Island mills advertised for men with large families (the children being workers too). The Lowell mills changed all that.[5] The family language continued, but the workers were single young women. The end of slavery was the final admission that a family system, even when the family was as thoroughly exploited as black families were, no longer made economic sense.

On the political side, the same process is visible. The British colonies in North America found it difficult to throw off the king because of the perpetuation of family imagery. As late as 1774 they petitioned George III "as the loving father of your whole people." It was Tom Paine's key role to break through this imagery. "Paine was able to help Americans to feel less filial and more, as it were, fraternal among themselves."[6] The colonies did establish a federal republic free from the trappings of monarchy. But the ironic twist which shows the residue of family imagery is that they then proceeded to proclaim George Washington "the father of his country."

The U.S. Constitution tried to save the citizens from paternalism and from arbitrary whims of political rulers. The system has worked better than most, but the founders did not envisage the growth of enormous corporations at the end of the nineteenth century. By then it was clearer that authority had passed from the father figure to the technical experts and political bureaucrats. There could have been other results, but what we eventually got was machinelike imagery in place of the paternalistic imagery. The family is not very visible in our political life except that when the impersonal organization does not solve the problems of crime, addiction, and general unhappiness, someone starts asking why the family is not working.[7]

On the economic front, the family ceased to be the unit of production, but it assumed the role of unit of consumption. Professional services and consumer goods are relentlessly pushed at the family in television advertising and elsewhere. The lament that the family is neglected today could hardly be more inaccurate in this sphere. The concern for family stability sounds disingenuous in the advertising of corporations who exhort families to spend more money than they have for the unnecessities of life. In this area the family might profit from a decent obscurity and absence of attention.

Professions

The missing piece which I now bring to bear on family history is the rise of the professional. The seventeenth and eighteenth centuries had doctors, lawyers, and ministers as the main professionals. There was great fluidity among the professions and an absence of any complicated credentialing system. The nineteenth century was the era of the explosion of a "professional class," each group trying to get hold of its own skill or knowledge that would guarantee a share in the new power. The concept of professional nearly reversed in meaning: from one who shares a special skill in the community to someone who can stand above the community to sell a skill for premium prices.[8]

The church professional tried to resist the change from rendering community service to being an individualistic technician. Nonetheless, the minister was still caught between talking of vocation to community service and having to scramble up the ladder of a career. Before 1800 the great majority of ministers stayed with one church throughout their lives; only a small number moved to as many as four congregations. In the next century the statistics on this point are the reverse. Church ministry, like the other professions, had become highly mobile. The individual minister had to keep moving up to larger and richer churches if his professional career were to be judged a success.[9]

The movement toward professionalization was almost exclusively male oriented. Men became the professionals, and women stayed at home with the children. Women were allowed into two sub-professions, teaching and nursing, because these were assumed to be works of the heart and not the head—a continuation of what a woman does at home.[10] Where women had their own ancient profession, midwifery, a bitter struggle was waged between the women and the new male profession. The midwives held their ground until the turn of this century but finally lost the battle (at least until it recently began again).

The main point I am getting at is that the professional developed outside of the family and to some extent in opposition to the family. Men became professionals; women had children. That simple statement should be kept in mind when it is regularly claimed that the family needs professional help. Is the very idea of "professional" sex-biased and class-biased? Is it possible that the form of the professions distorts their view of the family? Is the family's problem that professionals took away much of the power of the family and now lament the powerlessness of the family?

That line of questioning can go in the direction of Christopher Lasch's conspiracy theory. But, as I have said, professionals are here to stay. The twentieth century cannot get along without specialized skills and detailed knowledge. Any wholesale rejection of professionals is not a route of liberation for the poorer classes. We cannot return to an era before 1830, when the home and the professions were not split. But professional people could subject their assumptions and practices to greater self criticism than has generally been the case. The family, for its part, cannot afford to reject professional help; but where the relationship has problems, the fault is not all on the side of the family.

In particular, it is objectionable to assume that parents' non-involvement with a big institution is due to a lack of interest. A striking example of this point is the black family's relation to the school. Case workers and school teachers easily fall into the trap of assuming that black parents don't care about their children. "The irony, of course, is that they care too much—a kind of caring that limits their view of alternative strategies for moving forward; a blinding preoccupation that makes black parents and children more vulnerable to the modes of subtle and explicit exclusion they face in relation to schools."[11] In this case the conflict between the structure of the family and the structure of the school is inevitable, but it could also be fruitful. However, the professionals in the school system have to be acutely aware of the imbalance of power and of the fact that there may be deficiencies in the structure of the school.

I find even more objectionable the complaint that parenthood has not yet become a profession. If the word *professional* were only to mean "skilled" and "competent," then it would be desirable to have "professional" parents. But the word *professional* acquired a whole other set of meanings in the nineteenth century that trail along when professionals speak of professionalism. Those meanings—the separation of skill from intimacy, the protection of class privilege, the equation of community service with economic advantage—were developed in opposition to the family. The family fortunately has resisted the reduction of all human relationships to professional relations.

A recent book proclaims that "parenthood could be called the world's newest profession since it hasn't been considered a profession for very long."[12] As the authors' own accompanying quotations suggest, their statement is not very accurate. Since the invention of the modern professions there have always been people pushing motherhood and homemaking as professions. The great drive in the 1880s and 1890s did not succeed because women were rightfully suspicious of the whole business. The professionalization of parenthood (mother at home) was tied up with the move to sell the mother more devices and get her to worry about dust, germs, and untidiness. Perhaps it could be legitimate to talk about professionalizing the family but only if at the same time one asks how the professions intend to reacquire some of the values of intimacy, love, and non-marketable service. These are values which the professions may have to relearn from the family.

Conclusions

From the preceding discussion of the relation of family and professionals I would like to draw three conclusions concerning attempts to help the family.

1. Professionals have to examine their language and assumptions about the family. This statement may seem to be a truism: Of course, we all have to examine our attitudes all the time. But in this area there is an unusual structural

problem that has blocked the professional viewpoint. The professional was the one who moved in the direction of individual talent, rational knowledge, and carefully restrained emotion. The family has never shaped up well according to those standards. The families of some racial and ethnic groups, in particular, ran directly counter to a professional ideal. For example, when social workers confronted the Italian immigrant family at the end of the nineteenth century it was clear to the professionals that these families needed help.[13] But the families often resisted the kind of help that was offered. There may have been failure in understanding and communication on both sides. But I think that a greater responsibility lay on the side of the social workers; they were the ones who claimed to be experts. The immigrant families were often just fighting for their own survival.

The problem of possible bias from the professional side did not cease with the nineteenth century. Black family life has been especially misunderstood. Until the 1960s it was even assumed that there was no black family history. This is one of the reasons why the TV drama *Roots* was a revelation in this country: Most whites and even some blacks had been brought up to believe that slavery had systematically eliminated the black family. "The irony of the academic and sociopolitical assaults on black families lies in the fact that historically black families have been the central sustaining force of black culture."[14]

Discrimination against black families continues in more subtle ways today. The public prejudice against the unemployed and against welfare recipients is well known, and since a disproportionately large number of blacks are unemployed and therefore on welfare, black families bear the brunt of that prejudice. We see that prejudice in the stereotyped image of the cheating welfare mother, in the image of all welfare recipients as lazy and dishonest (though the facts overwhelmingly prove that most welfare recipients are in truly desperate straits). We see it in recent attempts to make all welfare mothers work—a move that defeats the original sensible purpose of the law: to give mothers freedom to raise their children.

Another instance of professional bias is the loaded phrase "broken family." A single parent trying to raise a family should not be burdened with this description. If the school, the parish, or the Little League treats a family as broken, that could lead to its breaking. One of the most remarkable family statistics is that 97% of children under 14 are living with one or both parents. That percentage is higher than at any time in our country's history. It is achieved, of course, only because millions of women and men are making heroic efforts under great economic pressure to keep the family unit intact. The frequent implication of the "broken family" phrase—that large numbers of black parents and poor white parents don't care about their children—is a vicious and unproved thesis.

2. The family help that professionals can give is limited and is always of questionable connections. This principle follows directly from the first. A little personal humility on the part of professionals would be appropriate, along with an acknowledgment that a professional is a representative of some large and intrusive organization. The professional may be getting paid by a university, a foundation, a church, or a state agency. These organizations may be more trustworthy than a transnational corporation, but from the family's viewpoint they all have enough weight and power to suffocate the family.

The professional is likely to protest that he or she is in

the work solely for the "client's" good. But professionals are caught up in the same economic system as everyone else. If they are employed by the state they bring some of the state's power with them. The state has, for instance, a legitimate interest in the rights and welfare of children within families. But the state and its representatives can become quite presumptuous about understanding the "best interests of the child."

Those of us who work with religious and educational agencies have an important role in being buffers between the family and the state. Without intermediary bodies the country might get to the point where the state licenses parents and decides how children should be raised. The professional workers, especially those not employed by the state, can provide environment and support that avoid direct encounter between family and state. In saying that professional help is always very limited I do not mean to disparage its importance. But even those of us who work for such small and relatively disinterested agencies as parishes and schools have to be aware of our own tangle of vested interests and overbearing institutional power.

3. The real, long-term help that the family needs is to recover some of its economic and political power. There may not be a great deal that professionals can do to solve this problem. However, in the loss of political and economic power the family's split with the emerging professional class was the culmination of the story. A recovery of political and economic power would include some restructuring of authority within the family and new economic cooperation between family and professions.

In becoming modernized the family in the United States displaced the father from any sort of patriarchal role. In the literature of the U.S., "Dad" has been either an absent figure or a character to be humored. The optimistic description of this pattern is the "democratic family." More likely what it represents is the absence of any consistent authority and thus a combination of maternal guidance, impersonal rules, and extra-family pressure.

In the past ten years we have been giving some new attention to fathering, a topic which now has appropriateness and context.[15] The neglected father was never the real culprit in women's struggle for liberation. Bringing back Father to the center is not a return to patriarchy but a recognition that the family needs an interpersonal base of authority rather than an impersonal authority. The family will be further strengthened as the brotherly and sisterly authority of children is recognized. Then we might realistically talk of democratic families in which differences remain between adults and children but everyone does participate in the exercise of authority.

The professional who is trying to help the family would do well to be aware of this changing authority pattern. The return of the father, women's liberation, and the children's-rights movement can all look dangerous to the family's health, and each can indeed be a threat. But for the emergence of a "post-modern" family we have to struggle through the dangerous transition so that father, mother, brother, and sister eventually occupy their rightful places in family authority. The professional's contribution is mostly confined to being an understanding mediator.

What the professional could do beyond that is look at his or her profession and examine its authority pattern. The professions even more than the family have adopted impersonal modes of authority. The ascribed authority of truth and service often veils the real pattern of bureaucracy and petty authoritarianism. The post-modern professions have to recover some of their ancient ideals of community service while developing new imagery of brotherhoods and sisterhoods. The professional's help to the family would be more congruent to family structure if professional organizations were brotherhoods/sisterhoods instead of bureaucracies. Urban legal communes or parish team ministries provide evidence on this point.

Finally, the family needs more economic power than it currently has. A first step is to acquire consumer power. Any cooperation across the lines of individual families is a help. Family professionals might be able to assist this movement. Families need a better tax break than they are getting from the government; family professionals should lead the way in this argument. Surely they know that on economic grounds alone it makes sense for the government tax policies to support the family. If a child is taken under the government's custody the bill is exorbitant. Non-parents might not like this proposal because they feel their taxes are already too high. But taxes go either to family aid or to more prisons, shelters, and orphanages. One thing sure is that the latter policy is more expensive.

The post-modern professional, reacquiring some of the ancient service ideal, has to work out new economic relations with the family. Parishes, schools, health clinics, and child-care centers ought to develop ways to help families without being so concerned about financial returns. The hope may seem romantic and unreal, but I am merely appealing to professionals to live up to the rhetoric they all use. Can we not tap some of the dedication that is still undoubtedly there? Should not a person making $100,000 a year have to make greater contributions to the family even to retain the name professional? Are there professionals who would be willing to work for less if the means were there and the effect were visible? The family does need legal, medical, psychological, and educational help. Organizations with a team or communal approach and with truly professional dedication can probably deliver the service for a lower price.

Church professionals have in the past given significant witness to unselfish dedication. I hope they can continue and strengthen this witness even if it's mostly a symbolic gesture in a world of great economic concentrations.

Despite their limitations, the professions could be a main ally of the family in its initial steps toward economic recovery. Eventually the family and the household have to take charge of their economic lives so that production is rooted in the household or in a network of households. Professional and family would then be closer together than they have been in the past century. The movement may take decades, but at least it is clear that healing the split between professions and family is the direction in which to move.

Notes

1. See Mary Jo Bane, *Here to Stay* (New York: Basic Books, 1976).
2. See James Axtell, *The School Upon a Hill: Education and Society in Colonial New England* (New Haven: Yale University Press, 1974).
3. Jane Howard, *Families* (New York: Simon & Schuster, 1978).
4. New York: Basic Books, 1977.

5. See Benita Eisler, ed., *The Lowell Offering* (Philadelphia: J.B. Lippincott, 1977).

6. Winthrop Jordan, "Familial Politics: Thomas Paine and the Killing of the King," *Journal of American History* 60 (1973):301.

7. See Michael Young and Peter Willmott, *The Symmetrical Family* (New York: Pantheon Books, 1973).

8. On the nineteenth century see Burton Bledstein, *The Culture of Professionalism* (New York: W.W. Norton, 1976).

9. Donald Scott, *From Office to Profession: The New England Ministry* (Philadelphia: University of Pennsylvania Press, 1978).

10. See Sheila Rothman, *Woman's Proper Place* (New York: Basic Books, 1978).

11. Sara Lawrence Lightfoot, *Worlds Apart: Relationships Between Families and Schools* (New York: Basic Books, 1978), p. 166.

12. William Granzig and Ellen Peck, *The Parent Test* (New York: Putnam & Sons, 1978), p. 15; on the nineteenth century see Barbara Ehrenreich and Deirdre English, *For Her Own Good* (Garden City, New York: Doubleday, 1978).

13. See Virginia Yans-McLaughlin, *Family and Community: Italian Immigrants in Buffalo 1880-1930* (Ithaca: Cornell University Press, 1977).

14. Lightfoot, p. 175.

15. For example, see Maureen Green, *Fathering* (New York: McGraw-Hill Book Co., 1977) and Eliot Daley, *Father Feelings* (New York: William Morrow, 1978).

For Further Reading

Burton Bledstein. *The Culture of Professionalism.* New York: W.W. Norton, 1976.

Kenneth Keniston. *All Our Children: The American Family Under Pressure.* New York: Basic Books, 1977.

Maria Harris, ed. *Parish Religious Education.* New York: Paulist Press, 1978.

Christopher Lasch. *Haven in a Heartless World.* New York: Basic Books, 1977.

Gabriel Moran. "Professionalization," *PACE*, No. 9, March, April, May, 1979.

Evelyn Eaton Whitehead, ed. *The Parish in Community and Ministry.* Notre Dame: University of Notre Dame Press, 1978.

Family Ministry:
Help for the Wounded Unicorn

by John R. McCall

John R. McCall, Ph. D., is a well-known clinical psychologist and the author of numerous works in religious education. His involvement in family ministry has long and varied roots. Currently he is Director of Human Services for the North Carolina State Department of Correction and is engaged in several projects involving ministry to families. Most recently his articles have appeared in The New Catholic World *and* Dimensions in Religious Education.

McCall describes the family as a unicorn that is deeply wounded in our time. He not only discusses the wounds but shows how the Church's family ministry, especially through well trained counselors, can help to heal those wounds.

The unicorn is a legendary animal with one horn. According to legend, the unicorn could use its single horn both to wound and to heal. I have often thought of the family as a unicorn, for it is in the family that we have our first experience of being wounded and being healed. Each of us undoubtedly remembers the terrible frustration of not being given the piece of candy we wanted, of not being able to keep our favorite truck, of not being able to run outdoors whenever we wanted to. But miraculous healing also took place in the family. Each of us can probably recall a time when our pain was almost too much to bear; yet a mother's kiss or a father's pat made it all better in the blinking of an eye. Yes, the family is a unicorn that can both wound and heal its members.

More and more of late, however, I have come to think of the family as a unicorn that is itself wounded and in need of healing. This is one of those periods in history when it has become more and more difficult for the family to achieve its goal of helping each member grow in the ability to love, to be loved, and to feel worthwhile. The family, after all, is just one organization among many: city and state and federal governments, the school system, the economic system, the social system—to name only a few. The complex and often conflicting pressures of many organizations have profoundly affected the family. Today's family is smaller, isolated, frantically busy, uprooted, fragmented. Where there were four or five children, now there are one or two. Many families are nuclear, separated from grandparents and other relatives; many of them are one-parent families. Moreover, many families today are constantly on the move as jobs pull the parents from city to city. And families are busier. In many families, both parents work, and even in smaller families, each member seems to live an independent life. I frequently hear members of families complain that they seldom have time to talk to one another. Outside activities scatter the family, and inside the home the television set often blocks communication. Meals used to be a time when the family got together, but today fast-food chains proliferate because families find it easier and, some even say, cheaper to eat a "Big Mac" than to prepare a meal at home.

Today's family is indeed a wounded unicorn. Parents experience frustration, confusion, harassment, guilt. And so they panic, fearing that they are not performing their most essential task in life—good parenting.

Fortunately, the churches are awakening to the problem. For example, the Roman Catholic bishops of the U.S.A. have decided to emphasize family ministry during the whole decade of the 1980s and have issued a plan of pastoral action for family ministry entitled "A Vision and a Strategy."

As a way of exploring both the problems and the opportunities facing family ministry in the 1980s, in this essay I want to point out some ways in which the family has been wounded and to suggest some areas in which the Church's family ministry can help to heal those wounds.

Establishing Support Systems

It is safe to say that a pervasive problem for today's families is the lack of support systems that modern society has largely taken away from them. Three types of family particularly come to mind.

The nuclear family. By definition, the nuclear family is a "stripped down" family consisting only of a mother, a father, and one or two children. This small family unit lacks broad-based support. Fifty years ago, by contrast, our families were more like clans. Our grandparents, aunts, and uncles usually lived nearby, and our many cousins were like brothers and sisters. In this typical extended family there were adults with special talents. Uncle Joe could repair anything; Uncle George could get anything for you, wholesale. Aunt Mary was as capable as a registered nurse; Aunt Elizabeth could sew up a storm (she could even make dresses for the prom). Because the adults in the extended family could help any children or parents in need, it was the extended family that healed.

Today, the Church can and must step in to supply that kind of help: by supplying well trained family ministers who can counsel, by putting the family in touch with many other already-existing support systems, by showing families how to minister to one another.

The mobile family. It is common now for a twelve-year-old to have attended three or four different schools and to have lived in five or six different locations since birth. Fifty years ago, families lived in the same neighborhood, and often in the same house, most of their lives. You didn't refer to a tree as the one in front of 301 Maple Street; you called it, say, "the Walshes' tree." These stable families not only had the extended family of kinfolk; they also had an extended support system which included the local parish church and school, the neighborhood organizations (often political), the city parks and recreation department (I can still smell the citronella at the band concert in the park), various parish societies, the American Legion, and other fraternal and civic groups—all of them sensitive to the needs of individual families.

The family that has moved five times in a few years lacks these helps from an extended family and from a broad-based support system. The Church's family ministry can supply a personal touch in an impersonal metropolis or suburb as it contacts families through expert ministers, refers families to existing support systems, and unites families into true neighborhood groups that in effect constitute an extended family.

The family whose parents work a distance from the home; the "service" family. Fifty years ago, sixty percent of the families made their living from farming. This meant that the majority of our families worked together every day and turned out products (grain, animals, and so on) that were visible, tangible. Even those children whose parents worked in a factory knew what products their parents were creating: Dad handled steel in a steel mill, for example. But today, less than five percent of our families make their living from farming; city children have little or no firsthand experience of family work; almost all parents work at a distance from the home. Moreover, many parents turn out no visible, tangible product that children can understand; because of technological advances, fewer and fewer people turn out a greater percentage of our products, while more and more people make their living providing services (such as those rendered by lawyers, travel agents, consultants). Today's children, then, who live in moderately affluent homes where little work seems to be done by anyone, have a hard time learning to be industrious and to enjoy real accomplishment. As a result, they easily fall into the luck ethic (your efforts don't really count; success is a matter of chance) or the welfare ethic (someone else will take care of your needs).

How can young children learn what work really is? How can they learn the thrill of achievement? They need to see their parents actually producing something; they need to share the efforts and a sense of accomplishment with their parents. In our experience, this is one of the most crucial problems facing the American family. A depressed youngster is often one who has succumbed to the luck ethic or the welfare ethic, for both these views encourage the depression that results from assuming that we have lost control of our lives.

How can the Church help in this battle? Frankly, there is no easy or complete answer. But anything it can do to create a true community of persons within the parish, within the neighborhood; anything it can do to make families more stable and to create genuine respect for and liking for cooperative work—anything it can do along those lines will be a step toward establishing the broad support systems that today's families need so desperately.

Setting Realistic Goals

All families have as their goal to help each member grow in the ability to love, to be loved, and to feel worthwhile. But each family also needs its own specific goals, and this goal-setting is one of the most essential steps in healthy family living. The Church can be of great help to families in this important area.

Unfortunately, some families set goals so high that achieving them is impossible. How many families, for example, can reasonably expect to amass a huge fortune, live in a mansion, take extended vacations in foreign places, send all the children to the most prestigious schools, and have them all turn out to be respected, famous, and wealthy? When such grandiose, unrealistic plans fold up, as they inevitably do, the family is unhappy, frustrated, and bitter; its only pleasure is to criticize others as a way of feeling superior.

The Church, through its family ministry, can help families establish realistic goals. A family ministry program that reflects a Christian set of values can, for example, help a family judge the true worth of such disparate items as honor, unselfish service, love, cars, swimming pools, TV sets, faith, friendship, loyalty, education, popularity, vacations. Competent family ministers can lead families—singly and in cooperating groups—to a realistic, down-to-earth self-appraisal of such gritty items as the money-making possibilities of parents and children, the true talents and shortcomings of the individual members, and long-held but unexamined family attitudes that may be harming the family.

When a family has set realistic goals for itself (goals that are high enough to be challenging but that are within reach too) and begins to work at attaining them, it begins to experience a sense of accomplishment, of success. The members feel worthwhile because their accomplishments bring them to their goals. In such a family it is easier to love, to be loved, to feel worthwhile.

This topic of realistic family attitudes leads us easily to a still larger area, the matter of perspective.

Gaining True Perspective

The popularity of the book and the movie *Roots* has illustrated vividly the importance of finding our origins—and this applies to the family as well as to individuals. No family can truly understand itself and grow in the ability to love and be loved and feel worthwhile unless it discovers its roots. And discovering our roots is part of the still-larger problem of seeing ourselves, our present identity, and our present problems *in true perspective*. Unfortunately, many families become so absorbed in their short-range problems that they lose all perspective.

The Church, through its family ministry, can do a great deal to help families gain a true perspective on themselves and their problems. In so doing, it can not only heal many wounds but prevent them. The Church can and should prepare family facilitators who can work with individual families or, more often, with clusters of three or four families who can help each other and thus provide the strengths of an extended family. A facilitator can help a family understand itself better, for example, by pointing out that every family is really three generations: the two families from which the parents came; the present generation of mother, father, and children; and the future generation that will be the offspring of this family's children. Families need to understand that they are influenced by preceding generations, even when they are separated geographically. In fact, the very absence of one's parents can sometimes control a family more strongly than if the parents were present. If they live close by, we can test our new ideas on them and get reactions; but if they are far away, we often settle for a fixed, rigid picture of them without testing the truth of that picture.

Again, the Church's facilitator, working with one or more families, can help families take an objective look at their present traumas. How did this present problem originate? Is it really as bad as it looks? How can the family members work together to solve it? For example, some families fail to realize that the parents (often because of the influence of their own parents) are perfectionists who therefore have unrealistically high expectations for themselves and their children. When inflation or gas short-ages or health problems or misunderstandings arise, and are not easily handled, the family is crushed because it is not living up to its own high expectations. Children become discouraged because they cannot please their parents; parents are equally unhappy. A good counselor can help a family analyze its perfectionist tendencies, put the problem in perspective, and thereby learn how to handle it in a healthy way.

Strategies to Avoid and Heal Trauma

A good family ministry program will of course use many resources that a relatively short essay such as this cannot even list, much less discuss in detail. I would like to mention, however, four important strategies that a counselor can help families to use in working on their problems.

Insight. Insight, in the sense in which I use the word here, is a family's understanding of its own emotional relationships. Insight is the greatest of all strategies for avoiding or healing trauma. When families become greatly disturbed, they lose the ability to see themselves clearly. The perceptive and well trained family counselor can help *all* the members of the family develop a deeper understanding of the emotional events that take place in a family—events that profoundly yet in unnoticed ways influence the course of family life.

The fourteen-year-old girl who runs away from home upsets the parents, who get even more strict with the younger siblings. When the family gains insight it will begin to understand why the fourteen-year-old is running away, and why the younger siblings are suffering doubly. It may even begin to grasp the fact that poor relationships are everyone's responsibility. Parents can suffer too. The process of helping a family grow in insight may be slow and difficult, especially in a society that has often failed to recognize the presence and the power of the emotions, but it is well worth the time and effort of all concerned.

Silence. The Church's family facilitator should be skilled in teaching families how to use silence as a way of avoiding and healing trauma, a way of actually benefiting from misunderstandings and confrontations. This is not the loud, punitive silence that families often use to crush their members but the fruitful, reflective silence of meditation and contemplation that we see Jesus and his disciples using in the Gospels.

All families need to be silent together at times. During the silent period, each family member has time to reflect on his or her own inner experience. This type of reflection can help family members grow in empathy as they learn to understand what motivates a brother or sister, a child or parent. Once they understand, they can feel one another's pain. The family that profits from its painful experiences by developing empathy for each member truly grows together. And this empathy helps prepare its children for future relationships when they themselves are husbands and wives, fathers and mothers.

Communication. As the Church trains its family facilitators, one of the main goals should be to show them how to help family members communicate with one another. Communication is the ability to share not only our thoughts but our feelings. In a psychological sense, communication is concerned with the process of connecting people in a union of understanding. As families learn to communicate better, they learn to avoid and to heal serious traumas. They need to know, too, that they must often master new ways of communicating as they go along. A couple with no children communicates differently from a couple with an infant child; when children reach the teen years, communication patterns within the whole family change.

A family facilitator skilled in the art of communication can help families to understand the three elements involved in communication: the relationships among family members; the meaning (messsage) transmitted or received; the process of communication itself.

1. Families are made up of members who have special *relationships* with one another. We have all experienced the misunderstandings among brothers and sisters, commonly referred to as sibling rivalry. And the misunderstandings among husbands and wives have given Neil Simon enough material to write a new comedy each year. When people are related as closely as family members are, communication is difficult precisely because these relationships are filled with overtones and undertones of feeling. Feelings, and not just ideas, are communicated when family members say things to one another. The first step toward improving communication in a family, then, is to help the members become more aware of the relationships among themselves. The youngest child feels that the older siblings get all the breaks. The older siblings feel that the "baby" gets all the breaks. The relationship itself interferes with communication.

2. And how many fights in the family could either be avoided or turned into profitable experiences if we were more skilled in *interpreting messages?* From our own experience we know that the cues, signs, and messages conveyed by one family member to another may be simple and

easy to understand—for example, a smile of loving approval a mother gives her child. Some messages, however,
are much more difficult to interpret. A husband uses his in-
dex finger to write in the dust on top of the coffee table a
message to his wife, "I love you, dear." How should the
wife understand this message? Is the husband telling her in
a cute way that he loves her, or is he calling attention to the
fact that she hasn't dusted in some time? Is it one of the
above, both of the above, or none of the above?

3. Finally, anyone helping families to interpret meanings should teach them to listen to their tones of voice. The
process of communication is itself dependent on the ability
of each participant to listen between the words and to be
aware of the hidden meanings he or she is communicating.
The intonation of a word or phrase may suggest irony, sar-
casm, or cynicism. The intensity of a communication may
also give it added meaning: A whisper can mean con-
spiratorial secrecy, while a shout can mean anger. Perhaps
even more important are the non-verbal cues. Long before
much was written on non-verbal communication, my
father summed it up for me in one of his humorous remarks.
When any member of the family would cast a displeased
glance at him, he would say, "Don't look at me in that tone
of voice." Unless it was a serious situation, that spark of
humor would often make us smile and help us get over our
grouch. Someone once said, "God gave us humor to keep us
from crying." Families that can laugh together can usually
learn to communicate.

What a wealth of knowledge the family facilitator can
bring to a family that is having problems with communication, and how many families would benefit from such instruction and facilitation!

Counseling by family members. It seems strange to say that family members should counsel other family members, but we are not speaking here of counseling in the technical sense. A recent book by Len Sperry and L.R. Hess, *Contact Counseling* (Reading, Massachusetts: Addison-Wesley Publishers, 1974), summarizes some proven means of improving interpersonal relationships and applies them to management. The family counselor can easily paraphrase the techniques given in the Sperry-Hess book and help the family apply them to itself. Three of them are especially valuable: keying, responding, and guiding. I will summarize them very briefly here.

Keying refers to skill in reading the members of one's family. In order to really key on another family member, we first have to give undivided attention to that person, both physically and psychologically. How often in families do we pay only half attention to each other? The title of a Broadway comedy highlighted this difficulty: *You Know I Can't Hear You When the Water's Running.* It's easy to say "Give undivided attention," but experienced counselors will tell you that concentrating on another person and giving him or her undivided attention is more tiring than digging a ditch. Another important part of keying is discernment: By paying attention to a person's meaning and goals, we learn to discern the true meaning of a comment or action. People don't always say what they mean, or mean what they say. The husband asks the wife, "How would you like a new wristwatch for your birthday?" She answers, "There are many more practical things I could use, if you're going to spend that much money." The husband has to discern her deeper meaning. She may want that watch very much but gives this mixed message. He can say, "You deserve the watch and whatever practical things you need besides."

The second technique in this type of interaction is responding. Having really given undivided attention and having tried to discern the true meaning and goals of the interaction, we now try to tell the other person what we think he or she meant. If we paid close attention and really perceived the meaning he or she tried to convey, the other person will acknowledge the accuracy of our perception and be grateful that we made the effort to understand. We will have taken a giant step in avoiding conflict, for perceiving another person's frame of reference is one of the greatest means of improving communication and deepening a relationship.

The third technique is guiding. In guiding, we try to share our frame of reference with each family member. Just as you had to shift to pick up the other person's frame of reference when you were keying, you now assume that the other person will be willing to listen to you. And usually that is so: Someone who feels understood and accepted is more willing to listen. When teenage sons and daughters have parents who can "key" and "respond" they are much more willing to accept guiding from these parents. What may appear even more strange, parents can accept guiding from teenage sons and daughters when these teenagers show that they too can "key" and "respond."

The present decade is gaining a new insight into the importance of family ministry. Or rather, under the Church's leadership we are regaining a basic insight of the early Church: We are seeing ourselves as the family of God. As a loving, caring family we are trying, through family ministry, to help all the members of our family to love, to be loved, and to feel worthwhile.

For Further Reading

Howells, John G., M.D. *Principles of Family Psychiatry.* New York: Brunner/Mazel, 1975.

Mahrer, Alvin R. *Experiencing.* New York: Brunner/ Mazel, 1978.

Satir, Virginia. *Peoplemaking.* Palo Alto, California: Science and Behavior Books, Inc., 1972.

Family Therapist:
An Emerging Role for Ministry

by Samuel M. Natale

Samuel M. Natale, D. Phil. (Oxon.) is associate professor of management at the College of Business Administration, St. John's University, Jamaica, New York. A psychologist, he has lectured and published widely in his field. His forthcoming book is entitled Loneliness and the Life Cycle *(Paulist Press).*

This essay is addressed to all those who have an interest in ministering to families in crisis. Dr. Natale describes some of the basic roles and techniques to be used by the pastoral counselor in such situations.

Recent psychological thinking, especially in the field of systems theory, confirms what common sense has told us all along: that the family is *the* institution primarily responsible for the development of its members, particularly in their formative years. The family mediates the "essential humanness" of the person and provides the arena for primary human experience. As Minuchin observes,

> In all cultures, the family imprints its members with selfhood. Human experience of identity has two elements: a sense of belonging and a sense of being separate. The laboratory in which these ingredients are mixed and dispensed is the family, the matrix of identity.[1]

As the basic social system, the family mediates between genetic endowments and cultural possibilities. It forms the most persistent influence on the human being and, in fact, as Theodore Lidz remarks,

> All subsequent experiences are perceived, understood and reacted to emotionally according to the foundations established within the family . . . . [These experiences become] so thoroughly incorporated in the child that they can be considered determinants of his constitutional makeup, difficult to differentiate from the genetically determined biological factors with which they interrelate.[2]

Current ecclesial thinking also reflects this appreciation of the family's central role. Several documents of Vatican II, for example, approach the family as a "school of deeper humanity" and as a "community of love."[3] The family is, accordingly, "the first and vital cell of society."[4]

This recent psychological thinking and ecclesial support have encouraged the Church's ministers to explore more fully how they can respond to the family as a whole. As such a minister I have written elsewhere[5] about some of the most basic problems which any minister encounters in dealing with families and about the need to reconceptualize our approach to the family as a system.[6] In this essay I would like to explore some of the basic roles and techniques of the pastoral counselor as they relate directly to family counseling, particularly in its difficult initial stage.

Whether they like it or not, ministers often move directly into the vortex of difficult situations. If they are to be even minimally effective they must mobilize the empathy, communication, and emotionally charged atmosphere of the family situation into a more open communication and sharing among the individual members.

Ministers who have worked with individuals on a one-to-one basis will immediately notice a major shift of emphasis when they begin to work with whole families. In any attempt at counseling, self-disclosure of the client is necessary. However, in family-systems counseling, the counselors enter an already-active series of communications and interactions which often all too clearly indicate many problems—as well as areas of secrecy. The ministers then have two initial tasks: 1) to point out and help reorganize the dysfunctional family communications; and 2) to facilitate general trust and communication by encouraging self-disclosure between and among family members.

Self-disclosure clearly helps evoke mutual trust. As Milton Mayerhoff points out, "The realization that 'he trusts me' has its own way of activating the person cared for to justify such trust and to trust himself to grow."[7] In order to build this trust, ministers must be careful to be neutral and must resist any effort of a family member to gain their support by "assuming" the ministers' conclusions—or their sectarian bias. The minister/counselor must maintain a certain critical distance to allow the members of the family group to explore and take risks.

It is important that the minister carefully observe family interactions so as to be a fresh observer without the usual benefit of a long history of information. Much direct and vital information can be gleaned from observing the *lived interactions and conflicts of the family in the here and now*. In our experience the stereotypical information a minister (or any counselor) may have about a family and its interactions is often detrimental to fresh listening and observing. Our stereotypes and assumptions often blind us to the behavior occurring right before our eyes.

Handling a problem in the presence of a whole family is often difficult for a minister who has been trained to deal with people individually and in confidence. It is axiomatic in systems thinking about family that the disturbance/dysfunction of one member manifests a *group* problem. Hence, instead of our more usual mode of listening privately to the distressed person and then advising, the family-oriented counselor invites the *entire family* to discuss the situation. After all, if the behavior of one member manifests the problems of the system, then only the members of the system can heal the dysfunction.

One of the most useful sources of information about interaction between family members is a home visit. Unfortunately, social workers and psychologists rarely use the home visit, though there is some attempt at developing the practice. Ministers, however, by role and tradition are often welcome in the homes of most people whom they counsel. Since it is not extraordinary to have the minister stop in, the family usually responds with little overt anxiety.

But at this point the minister's advantage seems to cease. Upon his or her entry into the household, the family usually pushes forward one individual as the "problem," but what the minister is actually facing is a complex dysfunctional *system*. In fact, so many interconnected events happen so rapidly that the bewildered minister is often tempted to withdraw from a systems approach and return to the more familiar one-to-one problem-solving encounter.

At such a time it might help the counselor to recall that the family appeals to the minister *only* when there is a crisis—like the person who phones the dentist only when an abscess is evident. This tendency to involve the counselor only during a crisis arises in part from the very nature of the family system. Since the family is a carefully interacting series of interlocking subsystems, problems seem at a minimum when there is a balance among elements. It is only when the balance can no longer be retained that a crisis emerges and a counselor is sought. This balance, we should mention, has both advantages and disadvantages. Positively, it integrates the varieties of personalities and needs within a family; negatively, it often prolongs an unfortunate situation.

The minister functions as both participant and observer. As observer, the minister always keeps a critical distance which enables him or her to critique "objectively." But as participant, the counselor is active and assertive, often verging on the confrontative. In fact, the minister often uses one of the most fruitful means of developing a family's insight: manipulating the environment so that confrontations and arguments emerge. (Only rarely, in my experience, is the role passive, and then only to allow the counselor/minister to absorb activities, statements, silences, secrets, and collusions.) All this participation and observation requires that the minister continually shift support and focus from one member to another.

This multi-faceted role may seem quite overwhelming—and sometimes it is. But if the minister with some training and supervision handles the situation sequentially, much effective change in the family system is possible. Where is the counselor to begin?

In the initial encounters the minister might usefully note such basic things as: Who sits where? Who speaks with whom? Who is the leader? Who seems left out? Who is identified as the problem? It is from this stuff of basic social observation that the minister will begin to sculpt a portrait of this particular family's style.

Throughout all these opening meetings the minister also begins to comment on some of the things observed. In fact, it is exactly in noting and confronting these behaviors that the minister begins to mobilize the family for change.

This catalyzing function is one part of a much broader function of the minister as a parenting figure. When the minister notes such things as alliances, for example, he or she is providing emotional security, warmth, and esteem in the family and is also guiding the family's resources toward cooperative rather than competitive or collusive interaction.

Together the minister and the family try to: 1) designate attitudes, behaviors, and interactions which presumably indicate some system within the family; 2) explore *why* family members feel and interact as they do, so that the minister and the family can discover more cooperative, creative ways of handling the core problem. For example, if the family has an alcoholic member, that destructive behavior has been supported, colluded with, denied, and displaced by certain members of that family. A new system of balancing must be evoked if there is to be a useful transformation of the situation.

The minister in this role as family counselor serves four fundamental functions. He or she: 1) enables the members of the family to appreciate reasonable goals by drawing their attention to various patterns and helps them articulate needed behavior changes; 2) supports, in a shifting way, all the members of the family; 3) is imaginative in finding ways to help them achieve their goals (e.g., the minister might encourage an argument between the parents or among the siblings); 4) constantly reevaluates the family's goals and outcomes. Through all of this, the minister remains an educator and a model by his or her *sensitivity* and care.

This first phase of family counseling aims at encouraging family members to explore their own attitudes, behaviors, and interactions within the family system. Since in this first phase the relationship between the family and the minister-as-counselor is something new, the minister must make his or her observations and comments with empathy and respect.[8] But—to repeat—this does not preclude the minister's direct action. For, while being supportive, the minister may also point up discrepancies and contradictions and continue, sometimes doggedly, reemphasizing them until he or she and the family find other ways to handle the family's problem.

In all this activity the minister is both *model* and

agent. He or she is a model for the family in openly observing what is transpiring and is an agent in imaginatively confronting and figuring out, with the family, new ways of improving a rigid and sadness-producing family system.

As time goes on, if the minister is to bring about behavior change and system manipulation, he or she must come to know the family's members as individuals with very specific needs and fears and with different levels of education, health, economic status, and social status.[9]

Since the initial phase of working with families is so heavily action-oriented, it is essential that the minister be *specific, immediate,* and *direct* in his or her comments. Much of the communication and action of the family members is necessarily ambiguous and unclear during the initial meetings. The minister's task is to eventually move this action into more direct and clearer statements. Moreover, if the feedback and responses from the helper are to be most useful and lead to clear understanding of the family subsystems, it is necessary to discriminate and point out various actions of family members carefully and immediately. This enables the family members themselves to observe the actual here and now of their interactions— many of which take place automatically and often just beyond the level of the family's immediate awareness. Direct comment from the minister forces the family to deal with its situation right now. This immediacy allows the helper to confront discrepancies between action and attitude and thereby raise to consciousness some of the destructive behaviors.[11]

Through all of these confusing roles, ministers who work with the total family must constantly remind themselves that as helpers their central roles are: 1) to interrupt harmful conflict within the family system and 2) to support the core of health. If the ministers' efforts are successful, family members will be growing in respect for individual differences within the family and will be critically reassessing family goals and values.

It should be clear by now that family counseling is no easy task. And since most ministerial persons are trained in the one-to-one encounter, it is no wonder that so many flee from dealing with the entire family. What are the ministers to use as a measuring stick of what is going on? The answer is the same as in dealing with an individual: Ultimately, the minister uses his or her own personal reactions as the barometer. Without gainsaying education and supervision (which are essential), a minister's own reactions to the family group's behaviors are the most useful indicator of the problems within a family. And it is his or her personal reaction which will provide clues to dealing with the problems.

A word certainly ought to be said about the sectarian attitude of the ministering person and of the family. More often than not, my experience has been that people who insist on a certain sectarian bias have a hidden agenda. It is crucial, then, that the minister, while fully standing his or her own ground, make it clear that when the family is in trouble, his or her role is not to evangelize or proselytize but to *describe* and *interpret*. Arguments among family members about what one member does or does not believe, or about how this individual does or does not act with regard to religion or to a specific church, invariably reflect a family disagreement on a much deeper level. The minister must try to help the family discover precisely why they believe that all family members must belong to the same religion and attend the same church. If the family system so desperately needs religious conformity, it is a fair bet that it also needs conformity on other levels; where exploration is aborted on one level, it is aborted on others too. The minister can help the family see that power is the real issue here; but a power used to manipulate and to demand conformity frequently limits growth, and often manifests a deeply pathological binding within a system.

For the religious person, power and authority always have a transcendent source. Unfortunately, though, both minister and lay people often confuse this power and authority with orthodoxy. For the minister-therapist, faith and conviction remain the dynamic basis of apostolic activity, but he or she will best express that faith and conviction by freeing family members to inquire and explore rather than by claiming them as members of a certain congregation.

Much more work needs to be done on how the minister's personal faith conviction and church membership are related to the way he or she goes about counseling. The interrelationships of religion and psychology remain badly in need of further empirical research.

Notes

1. S. Minuchin, *Families and Family Therapy* (Cambridge: Harvard University Press, 1974), p. 47.
2. "The Family as the Developmental Setting," in E. James Anthony et al., *The Child in His Family* (New York: John Wiley & Sons, 1970), p. 61.
3. See, for example, *Gaudium et Spes (Pastoral Constitution on the Church in the Modern World* in *The Documents of Vatican II*, ed. Walter M. Abbott (New York: America Press, 1966), pp.

201ff. (The phrases quoted are from nn. 52 and 47.)

4. *Apostolicam Actuositatem (Decree on the Apostolate of the Laity)* in Abbott, *The Documents of Vatican II*, pp. 41ff. (The phrase quoted is from n. 11.)

5. Samuel M. Natale, *Pastoral Counselling: Reflections and Concerns* (New York: Paulist Press, 1977).

6. Samuel M. Natale, "Religious Education and the Family," *Religious Education* 74 (1979):245-53.

7. *On Caring* (New York: Harper & Row, 1971), p. 22.

8. Samuel M. Natale, *An Experiment in Empathy* (Slough, England: National Foundation for Educational Research, 1972).

9. Brian Bolton and Stanford E. Rubin, "A Research Model for Rehabilitation Counselor Performance," *Rehabilitation Counseling Bulletin* 17 (1974):141-48.

10. Samuel M. Natale, "The Tribunal *Vetitum:* Limit Setting and Confrontation," *Studia Canonica* 12 (1978), #2.

Making It Alone:
The Single-Parent Family

by Gerri Kerr

Gerri Kerr is a lecturer and coordinator for ministry to the separated and divorced. In addition to being the director of early childhood education for her parish, she is on the Diocesan Board for Evangelization/Catechesis in Paterson, New Jersey, and is a member of the team to implement the bishops' plan for family ministry. Ms. Kerr resides with her four children in Long Valley, New Jersey.

In this essay she describes in some detail the stages of death and dying she went through in coping with a divorce and in raising four young children. She then traces her journey of regeneration and offers many practical strategies for the single parent in similar straits.

Watching the last trace of hope die in your marriage is an agonizing process. Sometimes it happens slowly in a prolonged erosion of relationship; other times it moves swiftly and abruptly to the point—the end point. However the breakup occurs, one thing is certain and is clearly understood by anyone who has experienced the pain of a divorce: It does not matter whether the divorce is a mutual decision or whether one spouse abruptly abandons the other. All that matters is the resulting finality—the fear, anxiety, and loneliness one has to face.

I am a single parent and one of the more than eight million divorced Catholics in this country today. More than one sixth of all children in our country are living in single-parent families, with the number constantly rising. These statistics reflect broad problems of society and speak to us of a reality from which we can no longer dissociate ourselves. Catholics as well as non-Catholics contribute to these growing statistics, and the problem clearly is not just religious but human. How are the fear, anxiety, and abandonment affecting the parents, the children, and the family unit? Is the road back to "wholeness" more difficult for Catholics? Where does one go, how does one cope, and what kinds of supports are most meaningful for those experiencing this transition? How does one best help children through this trauma? And how can the Church, and especially religious educators, help both children and parents through divorce and its aftermath?

Through reflecting on my own single parenting, an experience that has transformed my life both as a person and as a parent, I will attempt to share with you the hopes and struggles, joys and heartbreaks I have known. For the purposes of this essay I will be dealing with the situation of the fatherless home. Although this is the more common situation, the reverse situation is of course no less painful or traumatic for those involved.

The Transition: "By ending, we begin."

Nearly four years ago, my marriage came to a screeching halt after nine years. As the mother of four small children—ages one and one-half, four, seven, and eight—I was overwhelmed by fear, anxiety, and loneliness. Then I realized for the first time that supposedly happy, committed, Christian marriages break—with little warning—and that what one spouse no longer will handle, the other must.

This "transition trauma" has an explosive effect on all family members, and the vibrations seem endless. This family transition demands intense yet reflective exploration of innovative ways to meet the crisis. The struggle is painful as the conflict between "head" and "heart" becomes riotous at times. The remains and memories of the past—children, financial security, emotional investments, vows that were taken "till death do us part"—must now be fitted into the new framework of the present and into one's somewhat blurry view toward a future. Even when one is unable or unwilling to face the emotional realities involved, there is a whole legal process that jolts one into separating the past from the present.

The divorce experience is actually a "grief process." It is not a single process, nor is it clearly over at one particular point in time. "The divorce process is a multiple grief process. It involves mourning for the loss of not one relationship but many. In a divorce there is severance from the partner as husband or wife, as friend, as companion, as sexual partner, as provider, as person who kept the home, as one who shares responsibility for the children. This multiple loss process cannot be dealt with easily."[1] The "grief process" involves five stages: shock, denial, anger, depression, and acceptance.

Shock: Sometimes the practical needs of the children and of keeping a home bring one out of this initial stage. I can vividly recall being at the Shore during the early weeks of my separation, mechanically dressing the children into swimsuits and memorizing what each of them was wearing, yet the next day not remembering the ride to and from the beach.

Denial: This process has frequently begun unconsciously before the actual separation. "This can't be happening to me" plays games with memories that could have been clues to problems. Denial is characterized by such things as keeping the separation a secret from friends and relatives; it is enhanced by well-meaning neighbors and friends who avoid you in the supermarket or at Little League games. Denial is a significant stage in the grief process, for it allows one the time and space needed to get in touch with personal resources to face what lies ahead. "It carries with it, as do the other phases, the potential . . . for healing and growing through."[2] This stage comes to a positive close when the single parent no longer accepts standing alone at Little League games, confronts the neighbors in the supermarket, and expresses her need to be at one with others.

Anger: Of all the emotions involved in the grief process, anger is the most difficult to express. We have been socialized to believe that "nice people" do not get angry, or at least never express anger. When we do allow ourselves to unleash this freeing emotion, it is difficult if not impossible to separate it from the instantaneously ensuing guilt we feel. I can recall describing every detail of my anger to a dear priest friend. Besides feeling pounds lighter for sharing, I was touched by his ability to accept me completely at that moment, rage and all. His response, "I sure can understand why you'd feel that way," was the affirmation I desperately needed at that moment. It was the first of many learning experiences that told me that feelings cannot be judged—they come as they are—and that God loves us regardless. But what we do with those feelings can be the key to Christian growth and awareness. It was during those dark days, many of them, that I heard, really heard for the first time, the words of the Eucharistic Prayer: "Lord, by your cross and resurrection you have set us free. . . ." I identified strongly with the cross and lived in constant hope that through this struggle I too would grow to be free.

Depression: Depression is based on unexpressed or inexpressible feelings. "Yes, this is happening to me" is the reality, and sifting through the remnants of that reality moves one toward acceptance. During my family's transition I frequently felt hopeless.

> If you put together all the painful struggle that has been a part of two people trying to love each other, but, in the end, of failing, all of that pain and struggle cannot equal the terrible process, the trauma, the agony and the grief that follow when people begin to separate out two lives that they had once chosen to join.[3]

Often, after an emotionally and physically draining day, I would tell God how much I hated all of it—the uncertainty, the rage, the confusion, and the hostility, both mine and my children's—and how I did not want to be part of something so hard, lonely, and sad. Yet each morning all the problems were still there, and little by little the reality sank in: "It's here; this is it. *What* are you going to do with it?"

Acceptance: As the earliest beginnings of acceptance give rise to new life in and through experiences, life becomes bittersweet: bitter because you must allow the past to slip away, but sweet because there is, after all, some vision of a future. Even after accepting the breakup, the single parent must continue learning to cope with new situations on a practical, everyday level. More than anything in this world, I wanted to be a good parent. Having to make a go of it in the changed situation overwhelmed me, and yet it also motivated me to keep going. Family interactions lose their former spontaneity as the single parent and children find themselves in new roles, faced with situations and questions that are always painful and sometimes must be left unresolved.

What, for example, does an eight-year-old Cub Scout do when faced with the dilemma of entering a father/son cake-decorating contest when there is no father present? What does he do to hide the emptiness in the church pew on his First Communion Day? Or consider the preadolescent faced with the pressures of father/daughter dances or baseball games. It is accepted that the teenage daughter learns the intricacies of a male/female relationship through the feedback she gets from her father. What will she do if he is gone? The practical needs left unmet hit the preschooler also. The three-year-old cannot understand why Daddy can't fix her tricycle; she only knows that it is broken and that everyone else's dad is a fixer. She communicates her need in a question/statement: "My daddy's gonna fix my bike someday when he comes home?" When six-year-old Beth asks, "Did you guys have a fight one night and that's why Dad's not here anymore?" she gives only slight insight into the confusion and questions in her mind. And imagine what a child must be feeling as he says, "Tell Daddy if he comes back I won't be loud or noisy any more."

Whether one is a preschooler, a preadolescent, a teenager, or an adult, the loss of a parent creates emotional trauma. Because that trauma is so complex, the divorce experience requires abstract thinking of which the young child is incapable. The single parent must handle questions sensitively by answering them in a direct, non-complicated way, focusing on the child's feelings. In addition, the parent must be non-judgmental, for any attempts to pass judgment on the former spouse will only confuse the child, who needs the freedom to explore his or her own feelings. The former spouse remains "parent" to the child even when the marriage has ended. Perhaps the absent parent may avoid emotional interaction with the children because, cut off from contact with them, he has few clues to their feelings toward him and consequently is unsure of his role. When this happens, the remaining parent must help the children to cope with their feelings of rejection.

Obviously, then, the demands on the remaining parent are considerable. The single mother must "exert patience, objectivity, and self-control to an unusual degree, and all this at a period when she is subjected to emotional stresses of extraordinary intensity."[4]

Forming a Vision:
"If today you hear his voice, harden not your hearts."

Is the single-parent home the same as a "broken home"? Webster defines "broken" as "splintered" or "fractured."

Many two-parent families where hostility, fragmentation, frustration, and distrust prolong strife between parents are broken homes in the fullest sense. No matter how hard the parents work to prevent these negative attitudes from affecting their family life, their efforts are in vain. Children are sensitive human beings who react to their environment, whether they are witnesses to constant bickering or physical violence, chilled silences or token courtesies. If the parents are unhappy, the children will feel the vibrations in many ways and may well suffer later in life. The psyche of a child in two-parent home split by "emotional divorce" stands a very good chance of being fractured or splintered.

The single parent, on the other hand, is capable of building trust, exuding warmth and love, and thereby restoring wholeness to the family. Recognizing the need to be a good parent seems to be basic in this process. It has been said that the parent is "a psychological mirror the child uses to build his identity . . . and his whole life is affected by the conclusions he draws."[5] What complication does divorce pose for a child with just one parent to act as this mirror? A built-in problem is that a single parent is struggling with her own feelings of inadequacy, hostility, rage, rejection, fear, and loneliness. If she does not sift through these feelings and become comfortable with her own new image, she may reflect a distorted and unhealthy view to the children.

Sifting through these feelings at a shattered moment in life is no small task, but it must be done. A counselor, psychiatrist, or minister can perform a double service as guide and as recipient of the outpouring of troubled emotions. Counseling can be a mainstay through the rockiest of days, enabling the single parent to unburden the weight of inner turmoil which might otherwise be imposed on the children. This is not to say that children should not experience in some way the pain the single parent feels. On the contrary, children who witness only the single parent's strength are being denied the healing they need for their own hurt as well. There is a difference between allowing children to see pain and taking that pain out on them.

After a divorce the turning point in transferring acceptance into action comes through different means for different people. At a liturgy one day, the celebrant spoke to a small group of us about thanking God for what we had, rather than focusing on what we did not have. He talked about how cheated we sometimes feel as we see what everyone else has, yet fail to see the gifts that are ours. The feeling that had been steadily growing toward wholeness for nearly two years now had a sense of direction and urgency clearer than ever before. I was overwhelmed by thoughts of all my gifts in a life that I had been viewing as less than whole because of the breakup. For the first time I clearly saw that those gifts remained intact, untarnished: They were mine, they had been freely given, they were unbroken! My courage, my determination, and my acceptance of the challenge to be a fully alive, creative (though frightened) parent of an altered but whole family were never stronger than on that day. But one of the toughest questions I had to wrestle with was *how*. The positive approach required goal-setting, determination, and organization in a way that I had never been aware of before. I had to find new ways to understand and help the children, new ways to understand and strengthen myself, new ways to rebuild our life as a family.

One problem that concerned and confused me was that the children were so different now. They were sulky, they were hostile to each other and to me, and they always seemed distant. As a typical parent, an overly sensitive one at that point, I interpreted all their changed responses and behavior personally. I thought that they must be unhappy living with me and that I had lost my "authority" because I was a single parent. A friend who was giving a Parent Effectiveness Training course at that time encouraged me to join the group. Each week, walking into a room filled with couples pointed out how clearly uncomfortable I felt as a "single" in a "coupled" world—especially in the world of parenting. But I learned much in those eight weeks. It was good to know that since my children were doing many of the same things that children from two-parent families were doing, probably much of their behavior was attributable to normal maturing processes.

I learned about the communication skill of active listening, which helped me to "hear," in a non-judgmental way, what my children were saying. Active listening mirrors a person's words or actions, and it can be a turning point in family communications, a building block for family relationships. But it is also a skill through which one gains some very painful insights. The truth is that children experience the same grief process that divorced parents do. Shock, denial, anger, guilt, and depression are every bit as much a part of their healing process, although children have a way of bouncing back a bit more easily than adults do. It is extremely difficult to watch children react to a situation as painful as this, but the single parent can best support them by lovingly allowing them full ownership of their own feelings, being careful not to "buy into" the children's feelings or to be manipulated by them. Too often, a single parent, responding to the powerlessness and frustration of children's pain, will either sit in tearful unison with them or indulge them with some material goodies in an attempt to distract them from their feelings. What children need most at this time is the freedom to own their feelings, knowing how much the parent genuinely cares but also knowing that the parent will stay separate from their pain.

Through single parenting I have learned how beautiful and necessary true forgiveness is in a family. The ugly scenes of hostility, resentment, and anger that the older children act out are profoundly upsetting at times, but they can also be learning experiences. More than anything I want to provide my children with a loving atmosphere where they can evolve into the people they were made to be. It is an idealistic goal, but bringing it into reality is the beauty of the challenge.

The single parent must learn the art of being "tough" in a caring way. This allows the parent to separate herself from situations over which she has no control and to save emotional energy for situations where she can truly help. It is a part of the growth process and does wonders for the children as they attempt to own their own feelings, make their own mistakes, and take the responsibility for them as part of growing up. As a result of this separateness, I am far less concerned with things like "authority" in our family and much more concerned with values like mutual caring, sharing, and genuine concern for others.

Finding new ways to relate as a family wasn't always easy in the beginning, and many days ended with me in a quandary, wondering if my new ways of allowing the children to express themselves more openly were going to backfire. I heard such comments as "Boy, if he's slamming things around now, what will it be like for you when he's a teenager?" and "If you're parenting all alone, how will you handle that?" Perhaps there was something about the quality of the anger I was seeing that told me it just had to be allowed freedom of expression; or perhaps I was reminded of my own feelings, which no one could ever have stopped me from freely expressing. Whichever it was, my hunch was right: The worst of the storm is over, for the children were able to effectively unburden themselves and are now more "in-control" people. It must be remembered that feelings cannot be judged. They come as they are, and the best way to support children is not to repress their feelings but to help them channel those feelings.

In addition to finding better ways to understand and support the children, I had to take a hard look at myself. In setting any goals, one must function with some degree of objectivity. I gained this objectivity through another way of distancing myself from the family. My personal life had to broaden if I was to bring any positive self-concept to this family. In a time when so much revolves around "self," frequently to the point of excluding others, this seems a questionable route to follow. Yet there is a very precious balance to be found by developing self and then turning around to share the benefits of that self-fulfillment with others, especially when those others are your children. I realized that I could not cheerfully give to my children if I did not cheerfully provide for myself. And this attitude has taken weights off my children because they no longer have to feel responsible for me. I can recall the children's teachers telling me how much the children were concerned for me. I'm happy to be loved, of course, but as a choice, not as a burden. Also, as the children grow older and have lives of their own, I won't be resentful that my life is "over."

All things in life require a balance, and for me the balancer has always been prayerful reflection. This is a quiet time when one reflects on the events of the day without the annoyances of interruptions and frustrations, so that one can objectively evaluate one's progress. Prayerful reflection became a mainstay, a source of great peace, tranquility, and frequently of sadness as I saw what had gone right and what had gone wrong, the reasons why, and how I could make tomorrow better. In the earlier days especially, I often felt that the goals were mere dreams that would never reach reality. Being at times physically and emotionally unable to meet the needs of four small children has been difficult for me to accept. But learning to forgive myself for my shortcomings and learning to accept my own limitations has been a rewarding part of my own growth.

With a firmer understanding of my children and myself, I set about rebuilding our family. This meant, in part, a return to family customs that sometimes evoked painful memories. Birthdays once again became the joyful, special occasions our family had always celebrated. We resumed family outings—picnics, hikes, camping, all the activities that had made our family special to us—in a smaller but no less meaningful way. We found that we could not only remember all the growth and happiness of past years but could use our memories to build something new and meaningful.

We also had to handle practical problems. Finances were a major worry for me; the children, too, noticed the changes in our way of life. I can remember my oldest son bringing home a composition that he had written in school on "the most important thing that ever happened to me." His most important thing was that his dad didn't live with us any more, and that as a result of the separation, many things were changed. For instance, we never went to McDonald's any more. I saw this as a minor detail with some major implications.

I decided to work part time so that I could still experience the children's first burst through the door as they excitedly came home from school and showed me the day's work, and could still share in car-pooling for sports, nursery school, tap-dance lessons, and the like. Some friends considered my return to work purposeless, since I had to pay out a large portion of my income in day care for my preschooler. I had, however, several reasons for returning to work. Most important, I needed the psychological respite and objectivity provided by some time away from my problems. Two added benefits were that I prepared an updated resume and established a credit rating. I treasure this part of my life as a parent; I don't know that I'll always have it, but I'll enjoy it and thrive on it for as long as I can.

The single parent who returns to work must find ways to provide the children with good care at all times. The problems soon become evident when children are allowed to do as they please in the parent's absence—evident not only in incomplete homework and an untidy home, but in the children's attitudes. But a good sitter who is sensitive to the children's needs and shares the family's values can be a refreshing change of pace for both children and parent. In addition to providing good day care, the parent must realize when the children's need for her is more important than her own schedule. Recently, after six days of tryouts for cheerleading, Beth asked me to stay with her the day the final judging was done. It hadn't dawned on me what an important moment that would be for her—and for me—, and I was touched by the openness and honesty of our communication. That was one of many "million-dollar readings" which affirm the efforts of a single parent.

One of the best parts of belonging to a large, single-parent family is watching the children meet some of their needs in and through each other. The older children giving the younger children help in many ways has been a big help, something I have encouraged but not insisted upon. The beauty of it has been the spirit of closeness among them, possibly reinforced by their shared loss, but nevertheless the gesture of caring love. I can vividly recall Jennifer's third birthday party as Bobby, then ten and the oldest, rounded up a group of his friends to provide piggyback rides for the "babies." The boost to both of their egos was obvious.

Because of their extremely hectic life-styles, single-parent families seem, as a necessity and a blessing, to focus on shared responsibility. Everyone has something to contribute, from a five-year-old's peeling the carrots to the eleven-year-old's mowing the lawn or shoveling the snow. After coming as close as I did to thinking that our chances to be a real, fully functioning and alive family were over, I wanted to be sure my children understood that a family life is a shared effort that makes the family truly whole.

As a result of learning more about communication skills, I now view discipline as "the mechanics of home democracy." My approach to home democracy has been satisfying, for it allows the children to be part of the decision-making process. I learned that if we want our children to feel important and want to support their feelings of self-worth, we must allow their voices to be heard. Still, the single parent must be ready to take a firm stand when necessary. Children from a single-parent family must feel assured that someone is at the head of the ship. When our family cannot make decisions collectively, I do take the responsibility, firmly. Because there is flexibility in many areas, the areas where there is none stand apart as important.

The older children have shown interest and ability in baking and cooking, and on many weekend mornings I find ten-year-old Christopher supplied with a stack of his own pancakes. At the annual Cub Scout father/son cake-decorating contest this year, I asked him if he would like to enter the contest with me or prefer to pass it up, as he usually does. I was filled with secret pride as his eyes grew wide and he jumped with excitement at the thought of entering it with me. I wondered how the rest of the Scouting community would react to my coming as "father" and hoped we might make them realize the need for calling such functions "parent/child" instead of "father/son" or "mother/daughter." When my son won second place in the contest, he and I were very proud and surprised to find that the rest of the community accepted us as a "father/son" pair.

Living Out the Vision:
"This is the day the Lord has made;
let us rejoice and be glad."

As they wander through a seemingly endless dark tunnel, untold numbers of divorced Catholics are finding their way to the Ministry for Separated and Divorced Catholics. This flourishing ministry within the Church is an oasis of compassion and support that offers a sense of belonging to the Christian community—a feeling that the divorced person frequently does not have. After a divorce

> The sense of failure is especially acute among Catholics. . . . From their childhood religious education and social conditioning they are often convinced that they have failed as Christians and

did not cooperate with the grace of the
sacraments. . . . This explains why so many
divorced and separated Catholics drift away
from the Church at the time of marital break-up.[6]

This Ministry, through its activities, liturgies, and
members, has been a source of healing for my children and
me. The group's activities bend in many different yet
similar ways. At a recent seminar in the Paterson Diocese,
participants chose two workshops in the areas of communication skills as a tool for the single parent: one on the
annulment process, legal advice, and coping with
loneliness, the other on the male perspective on divorce.
There have been family days of reflection where child care
is provided by the area youth, who lead activities appropriate for the various age levels and thereby free the
adults for some sorely needed spiritual reflection. And
monthly meetings provide adult education for the divorced
parent by dealing with such topics as coping with a divorce,
morality, alcoholism, and divorce's psychological impact
on adolescents.

The Ministry's liturgies have been heartwarming
celebrations for our family, especially during those difficult
days, holidays! Last year at the family liturgy with the
Newark Archdiocese, Father Ed Holden asked all the
children why we get gifts at Christmas time when it is really
Jesus' birthday. It was my son Bobby, eleven, who responded "because Jesus is a little bit in each one of us." I
reflected on that for a very long time, remembering in particular our first Thanksgiving on our own: all in semi-
shock, finances very tight, legalities not squared away,
everything very hard, nothing "fair." Outside our front
door we found a large carton filled with food and many

treats. We never knew who left the box, but we began to explore how the Christian message goes: Jesus was a kind and caring person who lived a life of love, and the message he left us is to love one another as he would if he were still physically among us. The children and I have experienced that love in and through others in countless ways, a touching lesson at any age.

The Ministry has helped me to heal. Now it is my chance to turn to others and give back some of the many things I have received. I know what it's like to be broken and bruised, to feel incomplete and to wish tomorrow would never come. I've been there, and I'm not afraid to say to the many others who are following the same rough path, "Hey, if I made it, you can too."

As I work closely with divorced people, near to my heart are the significant others who helped me survive the initial stages of "transition trauma." The one characteristic of all of them was their belief in me. They didn't know how I would handle it, but they knew I would. They couldn't tell me the way, but they believed I would find one. They didn't know how to answer the children's questions, but they felt sure I'd answer them fine. They mirrored back to me strengths they knew I possessed—strengths that, in those months, I couldn't even remember I had. Not one of them said "I know how you feel"; they realized that everyone's divorce experience is uniquely personal. Rather, they said they didn't know how I felt but that they cared. Now I can respect that individuality in others. Although I've been there, my journey has been different. All I can hope to do is relate my experience and hope that some of it may help someone else.

What kinds of supports are available in the larger Christian community for single-parent families? My family had always been involved in religious education activities, and the local Christian community continued to sustain us with love and acceptance. But there is some perceptible change in attitude, if not in words or actions, after a couple's breakup. This difference bothered me, both because I couldn't define it and because I thought it might be a reflection of my own feelings about now being "different." One Sunday during the liturgy I understood the essence of what was happening. I realized at the sign of peace, as I hugged a member of my community who is especially dear to me, that her hug in return was one that knew it could only reach so far. She genuinely cared for me, but the tear in her eye told me she wondered where my experience had taken me, how I would survive it all, what my life must be like as a result, and whether what had happened to me could happen to her. Similar moments of profound insight have happened countless other times.

I question if some form of that same dynamic of not knowing how to respond is operative when separated and divorced people tell me, "I was always so active in my parish, but when my marriage broke up, no one even called." It is understandable how an already broken person would be totally crushed by such lack of Christian thoughtfulness and caring. In response to this insensitivity and hypocrisy many faithful Christians have walked away from the Church alienated.

Is the Christian community failing to respond to these needs because it itself cannot cope with pain? Have we been programmed to deal with feelings in certain ways only, and have the single parents confronted us with feelings we are not yet ready to talk about? Why is there an attitude among us that supporting single parents and the divorced, indeed welcoming them to full participation in liturgical worship, will in some way negate the Church's teaching on the indissolubility of marriage? The Church's teaching on divorce and its treatment of divorced persons are really separate issues. Divorced persons, like married ones, long to share in the fellowship of Christianity.

> The divorced want from the Church the assurance that the love they have for the Church is not questioned. They want to be free of the stereotypes that make them marked people in too many parish communities. They want to be able to share fully in the community of believers, sharing, as others do, both their gifts and their brokenness. . . . They want the kind of acceptance that Jesus gave to the woman at Jacob's well. . . .[7]

The problems faced can teach us much about what a true family is. Both single parents and married couples are searching for ways to bring Jesus' love and his invitation to life into their lives and the lives of others. This means that

> . . . we are no longer plagued with images of God that separate us from both the love he came to give us and from those we are called to love. It means that we no longer experience ourselves as dismembered and torn inside because we understand that it is in our human experience that God is revealed to us. It means that we can begin to carry our own responsibility for what the Church is and what it will be because we see the Church as a home shared by the human family as it searches for the meaning of life in the message of the Gospel. It means that divorce rates will only

be different if we link the sacredness of marriage and the sacredness of the person in the basic call to committed human friendship—a friendship rooted in the invitation of our baptism as Christians.[8]

Perhaps the Church must share the responsibility for many divorces. Is it significant that many who are now divorced were prepared for the sacrament of marriage as a "contract"? Now, as a result of our broader human and psychological understanding, we can dissolve many such marriages by the annulment process. We now understand marriage as a "covenant," which it truly should be. But do we push to the side those who never benefited from the broader, more meaningful interpretation of covenant? How do we rationalize all the pain and suffering of these faithful Catholics who tried and couldn't make marriage work as a contract? Having an inadequate focus for marriage preparation programs is forgivable; turning our backs on those who are the victims of these programs is not. Possibly these divorced Catholics, whose lives have been reshaped in many ways, may have something to say to the Church about lending assistance and adding insight to marriage-preparation programs. What a powerful, peaceful feeling to think that in some way our mistakes may improve someone else's chances!

What about the "inutility" of the Christian community? Child care is difficult, and frequently impossible, because of finances. As single parents are returning to the job market in an effort to survive, could some of the mothers and fathers, grandmothers and grandfathers lend a hand? If the Christian community made this endeavor a priority, or if it would at least become aware of the needs of single parents, wouldn't that be helpful as well as hopeful?

Making the Christian community sensitive to the many needs of single-parent families would be desirable for emotional as well as financial reasons. Rigid attitudes that must be reconsidered in the name of justice make life for single-parent families considerably more difficult. As Castelli has pointed out,

> Catholic schools continue to emphasize the intact family to the exclusion of other kinds despite the fact that one in four children in Catholic schools now comes from a single-parent family, roughly the same proportion found in public schools. Children are affected when their parents feel cut off from the Church.[9]

Frequently announcements for sacrament preparation programs in religious education say "Both parents must attend." In both A.V. materials and texts in religious education, families are nearly always represented as having two parents. This must cause twinges of hurt in children who have already suffered too much.

At a recent talk given at a Professional Day in the Paterson Diocese, Father Jim Young, Chaplain of the North American Conference for Separated and Divorced Catholics, encouraged the clergy to mention single-parent families in their homilies on Holy Family Sunday. He pointed out that this would not only make single-parent families feel that they belong in the parish but would be a sign to the rest of the Christian community that single-parent families are recognized and acknowledged by the parish priest as part of the full community of believers.

If ever there was confusion surrounding an issue and a "teachable moment" bypassed, it surely was Pope Paul's November 1977 statement on the American Church law

which automatically excommunicated divorced persons
who had remarried without a Church annulment.

> Sensitivity to the separated and divorced on the
> part of the total community could have grown
> and deepened, had time been taken to review the
> original meaning of this law. . . . Reviewing the
> impact on the families and friends of the
> separated and divorced . . . could have been heal-
> ing.[10]

It has been said that divorce can be a healthy solution
to an unhealthy situation. That is true, but divorce can be
much more. Divorce is a cram course in survival, physical
as well as emotional. Divorce can introduce us to things we
believed in but didn't know. Divorce can teach us that we
are all stronger than we ever dreamed and that we have
huge reservoirs of power for emergency use. Divorce can
teach us more each day about God's love, strength, and
guidance and how they are revealed to us through the experience of nearly not continuing, the experience of nearly
dying, because the journey looks all uphill. Divorce can
teach us the need for quiet time to hear the guidance of the
Spirit in our lives. Divorce can be an opportunity for new
life, a life vastly different from the one that went before.
Divorce can free us to find the priorities in our lives.
Divorce can free us to become the persons God created us to
be, free to become much more creative than ever before.

I like my creativity and I like what I am doing with it.
The children seem happy and are enjoying their childhood,
which is very important to me. The joys and the heartaches
are very much part of it, and I've learned to treasure both of
them because they are part of what makes us "real."

The children affirm my attempts at single parenting more than they know because they are thriving in our new family relationships. I know each of my children well and they know me, and what happens among us is a sacred relationship. They are four uniquely different, beautiful people, and I am humbled to be a part of each one's unfolding.

The effect of the fatherless home on their psyches concerns me, but all indicators tell me there is enough self-image to balance that out. Bobby, twelve, came home from school last week with another composition, "My Saddest Occasion." Yes, it was about his dad leaving our family, but it was more. He explained that he decided to write about it not just because it is the saddest thing that ever happened to him but also because his friend Jill had said that if he would, she would write about her dad's leaving, and "she really needed to write about it." Could this be peer ministry at age twelve?

I used to worry about the pain of the experience and how that might hurt the children, but now I believe that pain, lovingly and gently handled, can help form a more beautiful person, one who has integrated the joy and the pain of life, one who has become whole because of the nurturing and support given by a loving, caring family. We are not a broken family; we are faith-filled, hope-filled, and whole.

Notes

1. Paula Ripple, *The Pain and the Possibility* (Notre Dame: Ave Maria Press, 1978), p. 40.
2. Ibid.
3. Ibid.

4.   J. Louise Despert, *Children of Divorce* (Garden City, New York: Doubleday & Co., 1962), p. 14.
5.   Dorothy Corkville Briggs, *Your Child's Self-Esteem* (Garden City, New York: Doubleday & Co., 1970), p. 9.
6.   James Castelli, *What the Church Is Doing for Divorced and Remarried Catholics* (Chicago: Claretian Publications, 1978), p. 20.
7.   Ripple, p. 114.
8.   Ripple, p. 104.
9.   Castelli, p. 19.
10.   Ripple, p. 114.

For Further Reading

Bosco, Antoinette. *A Parent Alone.* West Mystic, Conn.: Twenty-Third Publications, 1978.

Briggs, Dorothy C. *Your Child's Self-Esteem.* New York: Doubleday & Co., 1970.

Castelli, James. *What the Church Is Doing for Divorced and Remarried Catholics.* Chicago: Claretian Publications, 1978.

Catoir, John. *Catholics and Broken Marriages.* Notre Dame: Ave Maria Press, 1979.

Despert, J. Louise. *Children of Divorce.* Garden City, New York: Doubleday & Co., 1962.

Gordon, Thomas. *Parent Effectiveness Training.* New York: The New American Library, 1975.

Krantzler, Mel. *Creative Divorce.* New York: The New American Library, 1974.

Ripple, Paula. *The Pain and the Possibility*. Notre Dame: Ave Maria Press, 1978.

Shepard, Morris, and Goldman, Gerald. *Divorced Dads*. Radnor, Pa.: Chilton Book Co., 1979.

Young, James Y. *Ministering to the Divorced Catholic*. Ramsey, New Jersey: Paulist Press, 1979.

Grandmothers, Aunts, "Aunts," and Godmothers

by Joanmarie Smith, CSJ

Joanmarie Smith, CSJ, is a daughter, sister, "aunt" and godmother. She is also Associate Professor of Philosophy at St. Joseph's College, Brooklyn, New York. She has co-authored Modeling God *and co-edited* Emerging Issues in Religious Education *and* Aesthetic Dimensions in Religious Education.

In this essay she insists that the extended family is still a fruitful ministry.

Defining the Family

When people ask me how my family is, they are referring to my unmarried sister who has an apartment in Brooklyn Heights and my mother who lives alone in Queens. We do not seem to fit any of the descriptions or definitions of family offered by the social scientists. We do not live under one roof, we do not provide for one another economically or educationally in any but the broadest sense, and we certainly do not provide for one another sexually. But who will say we are not "family"?

We are all, of course, being made aware that the situation of a husband and wife and their 2.7 children living alone in an attractive home is a dwindling phenomenon,[1] if in fact it ever existed in the numbers we projected. The divorce rate is rising, the birth rate is declining, the number of unmarried singles is increasing, and there is every reason to believe these trends have yet to peak. It seems, therefore, that while no particular definition of family endures, "family" endures. Yet any concept of family must include the notion of children. They are the condition of there being *anything* called family. There is, then, a legitimacy in focusing on relationships with children, even for those of us with no children in the household. For few among us are not grandmother, aunt, "aunt," or godmother to some child. The men, of course, are grandfathers, uncles, "uncles," or godfathers. But since I will be working for the most part out of my own experience I will concentrate on the female roles. In any case, it is my contention in this essay that there is a whole set of relationships which have yet to be tapped in family ministry programs.

"The Children of This World Are Wiser. . . ."

Contrary to all rumors and statistics, the extended family is alive and thriving. If you don't believe me, walk into a card store. Take note of all the different cards that are sold from the family birthday section. They include greetings for every relationship short of a "Happy birthday to my cousin twice removed by marriage." How is it that the social scientists and the family ministers have yet to discover what the market researchers have long known: that people will spend time and money cultivating relationships far beyond the nuclear family?

For some time the Bell Telephone people have had a most successful ad campaign where they implore us to "Reach out and touch someone." They illustrate their plea with engaging vignettes of old friends calling across a continent, children reporting their latest academic record to grandparents, and traveling husbands "touching" a newborn at home. People must be keeping in touch this way, or Bell could not afford to run the commercial.

Wandering into a gift shop at O'Hare Airport recently during a brief layover, I noticed that the big sellers were children's T-shirts with the inscription: "Grandma and Grandpa visited Chicago and all they bought me was this tee shirt." Grandparents were waiting in line to buy them! Department stores merrily ring up their cash registers on outrageously priced toys and clothes in "Grandmother Sections," and in many schools the picnics and entertainments of Grandparents' Day are eagerly awaited all year by children, parents, and grandparents.

This essay is a plea to the children of light to take a leaf from the children of this world.

1. Recognize and help others recognize this extended

network of relationships which nourish and are nourished by any family unit.

2. Minister to its needs—specifically through educational programs which cultivate the possibilities in these relationships.

Grandmothers

The grandmother has always played a significant role in the family. The term "grand" mother or "great" mother suggests the earth itself in its generating and nurturing roles. But the increased life span and other cultural modifications have revolutionized the image of grandmothers. First of all, they are younger. At the turn of the century, when the life expectancy of a woman was fifty years, a forty-eight-year-old grandmother was "old." Today, she is likely to be working and have fifteen to twenty more years of career ahead of her. She has, and will have, an economic security that is truly new in our society.

Secondly, in pre-film days children could only learn second or third hand of the celebrities in their parents' and grandparents' youth. My mother spoke of Eva Tangway and Woodrow Wilson, but they could never be more than vague historical figures for my sister and me. However, I find to my delight, and to the diminishment of a generation gap, that youngsters are being raised on the same films and TV programs that once thrilled me. The films and newsreels of the 30s and 40s and 50s are standard fare on daytime television. In informal surveys that I have made, *Gone with the Wind* ranks as Number One favorite film with high school freshmen through college seniors and, of course, it still attracts hordes of their elders whenever it is shown. Regardless of what else this might indicate about the state of our culture, a common pool of experience among two or three generations offers a source of communication which is unique to our time.

Yet there are marvelous aspects of grandparenthood that have persisted through these changes. Grandparents relativize the omnipotence and infallibility of parents. Margaret Mead makes this point in the article "Grandparents as Educators."

> The older generation's talk about one's own parents when they were children tends to reduce the tendency of adults to announce, 'My father would never have permitted me to. . .' And the fury of the young middle aged over disorders at the highschool is somewhat reduced by accounts of what happened a generation or two ago.[2]

Moreover, the pride and affection of grandparenthood remains, with more time and means to enjoy them. I sometimes wonder why parishes don't take advantage of this situation—why they don't follow the lead of the T-shirt makers. It would seem that an education program for "First-Time Grandparents" would be irresistible. They would not have the babysitting problems of parents, for example. And few people who have been subjected to the stories and pictures of new grandchildren could doubt their motivation.

Aunts

I remember my Aunt Edna taking my sister and me unexpectedly to a beach (we swam in our underclothes) and later to a Chinese restaurant (where we changed). The oldest we could have been was 2½ and 5 years. Some 40 years later I still remind my aunt of that happy day. Aunts (and uncles too, of course) are fresh breezes in family life. They introduce a healthy relativity into the structure of one's upbringing. They reenforce what is absolutely required for survival (Aunt Edna would not let us go *too* far into the surf), but they allow variations in the fulfillment of those requirements. They also allow exceptions. Aunts let you stay up past your bedtime and eat a piece of candy too close to supper. They let you *experience* being tired the next day and spoiling your appetite for supper—inadvertently building up some sense of why there are such rules in the first place.

Aunts also reenforce the perspective of grandparents. They too remember our parents as children, and it is even less likely to be an idealized memory. In addition they flesh out the possibility that siblings grow up to be nice people. In a parent's brother or sister one sees that sharing becomes easier, even spontaneous, through the years; that it becomes so pleasurable, in fact, that no one has to remind these grownups to "Give half to your sister."

Finally, one experiences oneself as special with aunts. Parents *have* to take care of you, and grandparents *have* to be interested. But you know that aunts love you, because they don't *have* to do anything that they do for you. When Aunt Edna took us out we had some vague sense of this. She communicated to us that we were very precious people.

"Aunts"

I am an "aunt" many times over. Some of my friends' children and nieces and nephews call me "Aunt Joanmarie." I have my suspicions that they recognize that so entitling me makes me putty in their hands. In this case *they* bestow upon *me* a sense of being special. It is a sense that has been captured in James Leigh Hunt's frequently quoted "Rondeau."

> Jenny kissed me when we met,
>   Jumping from the chair she sat in;
> Time, you thief, who love to get
>   Sweets into your list, put that in.
> Say I'm weary, say I'm sad,
>   Say that health and wealth have missed me.
> Say I'm growing old, but add
>   Jenny kissed me.

There is another source of satisfaction and pleasure in being an "aunt": It means that I am present to the adult members of the family as friend. In a beautiful chapter on friends in the book *Family*, Margaret Mead and Kent Heyman write:

> It may be said that civilization rests on the ability to make and keep friends outside the kin group and the group of those related through marriage, in a wider circle where friends can be chosen freely for their own sake. And the more complex a civilization becomes, the more emphasis will be placed on freely chosen associates, first as playmates and later as companions in study and work, as comrades in arms and as political allies. The more widely the net of friendship can be cast the better prepared each individual can be to create and live within a political community in which very large numbers of people feel secure and at home.[3]

All relationships other than friend refer to a biological or sociological bond. *Mother, sister, husband, teacher, priest* are scientific or social scientific categories, but *friend* seems more of an aesthetic designation. The oft-quoted "Nature gives us our relatives but we create our friends" bears this out. If art is nature transformed,[4] then friendship is the transformation of human relationships by choice and genius into bonds that are delightful and fulfilling. Friendships can emerge from the natural relationships, of course, and it can be argued that that is the fulfillment of those relationships. When we become friends with our parents, our spouses, our teachers, and our priests those relationships are recreated in such a way as both to fulfill their possibilities and transcend their limitations. When my sister and I became friends, our friendship had a unique base in communal experiences. We can examine in our conversation incidents and intimacies common to our growing up that no other friendship can offer. At the same time the edge has been taken off our sibling rivalry. Moreover, we bring to the relationship our other friends who have now, in many cases, become our mutual friends, enhancing the process of cross fertilization, extending the network in which we can feel "at home."

Friends usually share their children by making the friend an honorary sibling so that the children can refer to her as "aunt." Sometimes it is only as the children grow that they realize that there are quotation marks around the title. But at the same time the children are being initiated into the realization that relationships outside the family can be as enduring as those within it. I submit that such a realization is a religious education upon which the survival of our planet depends.

Godmothers

In the new rite of Baptism there is something of a downgrading of the role of godparents. It is in reality, I guess, an upgrading of the parents' role, but since I will never be a parent and I *am* a godmother, I read the rite with that prejudice.

In other languages—Italian and Spanish, for example—the word for godmother is co-mother; the emphasis is upon relationship between the parents and godparents. They are to assist the parents. They are to co-parent. And in fact this is also the emphasis of the Church in the single but awesome question addressed to the godparents during the Baptism: "Are you ready to help the parents of this child in their duty as Christian parents?" This concept bears out the way godparents are selected. They are usually friends of the parents—frequently related to one or both of the parents but almost always friends too. Indeed, it has become common practice to ask the best man and maid of honor at one's wedding to be the sponsor of the firstborn. It is, I think, an appropriate practice. Those persons selected as "best" to represent the community of family and friends as witnesses to the celebration of the marriage are now asked to continue their supportive role as the marriage bears fruit.

If other languages and the rites (if not the law) of the Church emphasize the relationship of the godparents to the parents, fairy tales have emphasized the relationship with the child. The very term *fairy godmother* conjures up a person from whom all good things come. It is the fairy godmother who intervenes in hardship and sorrow, not simply to make the difficulties bearable but to resolve them in a manner beyond our wildest imaginings. Cinderella, the most famous and most universal of fairy tales, has provided an image of a godmother that is directly modeled on our image of the Deity itself.

Peter Berger lists as the first of his "Rumor of Angels" or signals of Transcendence the underlying order of the universe in a mother's calming of a fretting child with "It's all right. Everything is all right."[5] He does not cite as an additional rumor or signal the conventional role of godmothers. But I think he might have. Godmothers, even the least religious of them, are expected to show up at special moments with extra-special surprise gifts. They are a resource against the dailyness of family living. While all the children in a family share the same parents, grandparents, aunts and uncles, they rarely share the same godmother. For that woman they are singular and unique in a way children can understand. Godparents don't have to be fair to the other children in the family. It is an accepted fact that the godchild has a privileged relationship to this adult that is not a source of envy because each child ideally has an analogously privileged relationship that he or she does not have to share with brothers and sisters.

Woody Allen as the character in his film *Manhattan* is accused of thinking and acting like God. He answers, "Well, you have to model yourself on someone." It seems that the godparent relationship is so peculiarly structured that only God provides the model.

The Extended Family Ministry

Nothing exists outside of community. More and more we are realizing that things and persons do not *have* relationships: They *are* their relationships. Lewis Thomas makes this point in a discussion of cloning. If you really wanted to clone another person you would have to clone the entire environment that nourished that person to be who he or she is. The parents must be cloned, obviously. But, as Thomas says,

> This is only the beginning. It is the whole family that really influences the way a person turns out, not just the parents according to current psychiatric thinking. Clone the family.

> Then what? The way each member of the family develops has already been determined by the environment set around him, and this environment is more people, people outside the family, schoolmates, acquaintances, lovers, enemies, car-pool partners even, in special circumstances, peculiar strangers across the aisle on the subway. Find them and clone them.

> But there is no end to the protocol. Each of the outer contacts has his own surrounding family and his and their outer contacts. Clone them all.

> To do the thing properly, with any hope of ending up with a genuine duplicate of a single person, you really have no choice. You must clone the whole world, no less.[6]

Thomas' ideas on cloning are a dramatic recognition of the fact that no one, nor any couple, nor any nuclear family, can be ministered to outside the network of relationships that sustain and nourish these units. And while it is patently impossible to address car-pool partners and strangers across subway aisles in our ministry, it is the thesis of this essay that there are persons available and motivated to whom we should be attending.

The easiest way to do so is to provide opportunities for ritual recognition of these relationships. Let parishes, following the lead of other organizations, have grandparent days and grandparent liturgies. (Just as there are enough children to go around, so there are enough persons who can act as "grandparents" if a child has none or if they live too far away.) There can be a similar setup for godparents. And in fact any group in the parish whose membership is composed of the unmarried and/or the childless—most especially religious orders—might initiate a "Favorite Children" program where the Church would be the patron of a program analogous to that fostered by Big Brothers.

Providing a special catechesis for these relationships might require time and effort. Yet it seems feasible, for example, to recruit "old" grandparents to prepare "new" grandparents for their roles. Or a DRE could promote an updating on what and how grandchildren learn religion today. Such a course might attract many elder members of a parish and have the effect of a general theological updating.

Some educational opportunities are so obvious that I marvel that they have not been exploited sooner. To concentrate pre-Cana and Cana courses on the couple alone is to miss the occasion to nourish those relationships which can help to make or break a marriage. Shouldn't there be at least an "In-law Night" and "A Best Man and Best Woman Night" in any marriage-preparation series?

Finally, being selected as a godparent can certainly be considered a "teachable moment." The affirmation implied is a unique motivation to learn what might be involved in that query, "Are you ready to help the parents of this child in their duty as Christian parents?" Yet to my knowledge there are few, if any, parishes that ask god-parents to prepare in any way to answer the question. There are programs for parents, of course. There are even books and booklets that are distributed to the parents which nicely outline the theology of Baptism in the context of the entire sacramental system. It is my contention, however, as it has been through this essay, that religious educators are overlooking a segment of the network of persons who will foster or frustrate the child's development in the faith community. Where are the godmother programs? Where are the godmother books?

In sum: The question is not whether the extended family exists. It does. The question is rather, Can any family ministry be really effective which does not address itself to this extended family? I think it cannot.

Notes

1.   Maria Harris, "Issues to Be Faced in the Future," *The Cathechist*, Nov.-Dec. 1978, pp. 12, 35.

2.   Margaret Mead, "Grandparents As Educators," *Teachers College Record*, Dec. 1974, p. 247.

3.   Margaret Mead and Kent Heyman, *Family* (New York: Doubleday, 1965), p. 106.

4.   John Dewey, *Art As Experience* (New York: Minton, Balch & Co., 1934), p. 79.

5.   Peter Berger, *A Rumor of Angels* (New York: Doubleday, 1969), p. 69.

6.   Lewis Thomas, *The Medusa and the Snail* (New York: Viking Press, 1979), pp. 54-55.

For Further Reading

Durka, Gloria, and Smith, Joanmarie, eds. *Emerging Issues in Religious Education.* New York: Paulist Press, 1976.

Harris, Maria, ed. *Parish Religious Education.* New York: Paulist Press, 1978.

Mead, Margaret. *Blackberry Winter: My Earlier Years.* New York: Morrow, 1972.

Moran, Gabriel. *Education Toward Adulthood.* New York: Paulist Press, 1979.

The Family, Heart of Liturgy

by Bernard Cooke and Pauline Turner

Pauline Turner, a sociologist, and Bernard Cooke, a theologian, both teach at the University of Calgary. Both have published in their respective fields, and both have been actively involved in liturgical and ministerial renewal at the local level. Much of their current interest in family ministry is derived from their involvement in the religious education of their young daughter. Bernard's latest major work is Ministry to Word and Sacraments.

Here they describe family life as liturgy and the home as a locus of celebration.

One of the most striking features of the first two generations of Christians was their attitude to worship and liturgy. In their distinctively Christian worship—which as they distanced themselves more and more from Judaism became their only worship—they broke quite consciously with the *cultic* attitudes that characterized their pre-Christian religious lives. In the cultic mentality the sphere of the religious or "the sacred" is special and apart from ordinary life: There are sacred times and festivals, sacred places where sacred actions are performed, and sacred personnel who perform these formally sacred acts. But earliest Christianity had no such priests, nor temples, nor sacrifices.

At first glance this might seem to indicate some loss of a sense of the sacred; but just the opposite was true. With the death and resurrection of Jesus there was nothing in the lives and persons of those who accepted him in faith that was not sacred. The entire life of a Christian is sanctified by the presence of Christ's Spirit; so Paul refers to Christians simply as "the saints." Thus, when Christians gathered together they celebrated the saving presence of Christ and his Spirit in the totality of their lives.

These early Christians did have a certain number of symbolic actions, but these were rituals that flowed logically from the Christians' existence in community. New members were received into the community in the ritual act of initiation through baptizing. Regularly the members of a Christian community gathered "to break the bread," what today we call the Eucharist, in order to glorify God gratefully for all he is, for all he had done to them through his Servant Jesus, for the triumph of life over death. Such eucharistic celebration came into being very early, not as a cultic act in addition to the remainder of their lives, but as a family gathering that celebrated what the rest of their lives had now become—and as Paul reminded them, it was the totality of their lives that was the sacrifice God desired of them.

The Hebrew Bible still held a privileged place for these early Christians, but it was not seen as the exclusive "word of God." Rather, the basic human experience of being the people they were—privileged people because of their exposure to the Gospel and the action of the Spirit—spoke to them about the saving presence of God in the risen Christ. Consequently, in their liturgical gatherings it was the remembered words of Jesus and the memories of the earliest Christian experience of Jesus (what grew into the New Testament literature) that were recalled for instruction and imitation.

Not all human experience is equally significant, so quite naturally it was the "peak experiences," key events such as birth and death and marriage and success or failure and the need for decision, that received special celebration in these early Christian communities. It was to such peak experiences in the life of Jesus himself that they turned with particular interest, seeing the way in which those experiences revealed the relation of the human Jesus to God. It was in the following of Jesus, in discipleship, that they sought to bring their own lives into relation to his Father. Without putting it in precisely those terms, they sought to make the entirety of their human existing *sacred;* for "sacredness" means essentially "proximity to the divine." It would be more accurate to say that they recognized that it was God himself, in his Word and his Spirit, who by his proximity to them in personal presence sacralized their lives. This was why the first letter of Peter would refer to them as "a holy priesthood offering spiritual sacrifices acceptable to God." It was this culminating "great deed" of

God that they glorified in the prophetic proclamation of the eucharistic prayer.

In this early stage, Christian life was rooted in ordinariness; it was basically familial in structure and setting and tone; it celebrated the "simple joys" of humans—the birth of a child, the beauty of nature, the love of a friend—and celebrated, too, suffering for justice' sake and witness in death to the Gospel.

Modern research, especially in psychology, can help us define more sharply the sanctifying role of such community celebrations of life in early Christianity. Psychologists—and the name of Abraham Maslow is probably the most prominent in this regard—have clarified the way in which certain experiences, because they are more keenly felt and more challenging and fuller in meaning, stand out from the ordinary course of our awareness and interpret the meaning and purpose of the rest. Some of these "peak experiences" might be anticipated; others are unexpected. "Falling in love," for example, functions quite regularly to recast the whole context of a person's consciousness, to give the whole of life a different meaning; on the other hand, the experience of staring death in the face in an automobile accident might put everything into a new perspective.

To the experiences that each one of us has as an individual must be added those "peak experiences" we share in by vicarious experience. As we watch Shakespeare's *Romeo and Juliet* or Prokofiev's ballet version of it, we are caught up into the destiny-shaping events on the stage, identify with them to some extent, and so learn another facet of the meaning of human existence. Again, a child can come to appreciate the spirit of Christianity by enjoying the musical *Godspell* or watching Menotti's *Amahl and the Night Visitors.*

The impact of such happenings is, however, relative to a number of factors: Persons are more or less sensitive to human relationships; persons are more or less perceptive about the implications of danger or failure or even death; persons are more or less concerned about their lives' having meaning or purpose. Varying backgrounds and cultural heritages can lead people to "read" such experiences quite differently: The birth of a daughter might mean for one woman a moment of great joy and fulfillment; for another woman it might be a moment of keenly felt disappointment and a failure because she had not borne a son.

What this says, then, is that there is a need to educate persons for such key experiences if we wish them to interpret them in a way that contributes to their personal growth. People are aware of this need, even if only implicitly. Each culture has its own ways of imparting to the young its view of the meaning of those universal and impact-ful happenings. Our day is no exception; or perhaps in our day the need is accentuated, because the range and rapidity of people's exposure to various experiences is so greatly increased. There is a clear need for our various educational agents—home, school, church, communications media—to help people develop the capacity to interpret more accurately and profoundly the meaning of their life experience. Only if this need is filled will men and women have full opportunity to become persons, to grow into response-able beings.

Celebration plays an essential role in such education. It is in celebrating some happening that one really understands it as positively meaningful for oneself. It is in entering into a celebration that one interiorizes the value judgment that is being transmitted by a community as it celebrates. It is in celebration that the individual can give voice to his or her innermost attitude toward life, and do so in a manner that finds identification with the attitudes of others. Or, to put it all another way, it is in celebrating that humans become most genuinely and deeply a community.

Celebration, in this basic but profound sense, is specially appropriate to Christianity: No insight of Christian faith is more central than the realization that one's self, one's life, is a good and precious thing given by a loving God. Gratitude for and happy acceptance of life is fundamental to Christian worship; it *is* worship, for it is acknowledgment of that God who really is, the only God, the God revealed to us in Jesus the Christ. Without this kind of open, grateful grasping of life with all its challenges and joys and risks there can be no worship worthy of the name "Christian." This is what liturgy is meant to be.

The Home as Hermeneutic

To say that the home, the family community is the principal context for the kind of celebration we just described, the principal context or hermeneutic for this ongoing interpretation of experience, is almost a truism. Yet there is often a value in saying the obvious, particularly when the obvious is largely overlooked. So let us quickly look at the way in which the home is the privileged place for interpreting experience, the privileged place of celebration. And it might be good to admit in advance that the following description of the family's role is idealistic—but does not Acts 2 tell us that we Christians are to have visions and dream dreams?

The home is unparalleled as a situation for sharing and educating life's experiences. It is in the home that parents introduce their children into the meaning of human life, lead them into the process of their own self-identification, and help them to interpret the often-puzzling happenings of their days and young years. But the home also allows the sharing of insights between husband and wife, a sharing that enriches each one's understanding of life, a sharing that opens up unexpected capacities for appreciating the ordinary and the daily. And in any loving family there is the exciting and youth-preserving process in which the growing children provide for their parents new visions of what it means to be human, new hopes, new horizons of achievement.

As families beget families, not just biologically but spiritually, human culture is transmitted. At the heart of this continuing and evolving current of life and experience one can find a "wisdom," a distillation of understanding about what it means to be human. This wisdom, a complex of knowledge and values and ideals and practical know-how, is what lies beyond the way in which individuals and groups make their choices, create their art, build their cities, spend their time and money and energy, and deal with one another in trusting love or fear-filled hostility. Day after day, usually in subtle and scarcely perceptible fashion, it is this kind of wisdom that is communicated in family life. For the most part, it is lived rather than spoken.

Yet it is critically important that it be spoken, that it be explicitly recognized, so that it can interact with the experiences through which the members of the family are passing—either to reinforce or to challenge the prevailing wisdom of the day. This is particularly relevant in a Christian family, because in that situation a new dimension of "interpretation" is meant to be introduced, the dimension of faith. Any Christian parent who has tried to share this faith view with growing children, or for that matter tried to live out this faith as an example for children, knows how difficult this is. St. Paul, centuries ago, told the Corinthians in one of his letters why: Christian faith is built on a wisdom that "the world" considers plain foolishness; for how can any intelligent person accept the fact that the key to happiness and life is the folly of the cross of Christ?

But it is precisely this paradoxical vision of Christian faith that is needed if we are to be thoroughly realistic about the meaning of our lives. And our lives do have *some* meaning for us. The daily experiences, and particularly the more significant happenings, do function as a *word* to us: They tell us about our importance or lack of importance; they disclose our destiny to us and shape it; in implicit form they tell us about some ultimate reality (God) that is either threatening or compassionate. One can really say—and some theologians today are saying—that the sequence of experiences that make up our human lives is the most basic "word of God" that reveals to us what it means to be human and what kind of god is the ultimate force in our universe.

The problem is that our lives are, at least in part, an ambiguous word, a message that is hard to read accurately. Let us say, for instance, that I experience rejection by some of my friends because I will not enter into a shady business deal with them. I can interpret this rejection as something that happens because these acquaintances are unscrupulous, or I can interpret it as something that happens (and probably shouldn't happen) because I am unrealistically and foolishly scrupulous. In such instances how am I to judge? What is the correct reading of the situation?

We need another source of interpretation from outside our experience, another "wisdom" to help us find the true meaning of our lives. And it is here that the revelation given us by God in Jesus Christ, a revelation we take in faith, provides the needed guidance. Not that we then get ready-made answers to life. Jesus himself needed to grow "in wisdom and nature and grace"; like us, he had to learn how to respond honestly to the demands and challenges of each new situation; he had to make choices with the risks that come in facing an uncertain future. But he did so in the light of his experience of who God really is, his Father. So those who call themselves "Christian" try to understand their life experiences in the light of this same view of God, and try to respond to the challenge of this "word of God."

Now it would be an error to claim that the family by itself can teach people how to interpret their daily experiences in this faith way. We need the various ministries that, in the full context of Christian community, help shape our faith: detailed catechetical instruction, carefully celebrated liturgies within which the homily functions to clarify and to encourage, vital parish life that provides a context for concerned action along lines of social justice. All of these provide guidance as we try to understand how Christian faith gives us a special vision of the meaning of human existence. But the family situation has one great advantage: It can provide Christian faith-understanding to daily experiences *as these experiences are happening*, so that faith insight can become an intrinsic part of the experiences themselves.

This is part of the process which all parents recognize: the almost incessant questioning carried on by children as they grow from infancy toward adolescence (and which, if responded to, can continue through adolescence), questions about their own origins, about the "way things used to be," about the reasons behind people's behavior, about the identity of countless bugs and plants and other growing

things. There are also the more anguished questions about
their own worth, about the value to be placed on their
achievements, about the way their parents really view
them—questions which are seeking some denial of their
own (at times) self depreciation, their own feelings of
failure, their own worries about being unlovable. And
always the most persistent question—why?

It is above all in response to "why?", in response to its
search for *final* reasons, that the understandings coming
with Christian faith are appropriate—though they are also
blessedly appropriate to the questions of self-worth. The
ultimate "whys" can never be given a completely satisfac-
tory answer apart from some form of faith. And it is when
Christian faith is explained as a divinely given reply to these
deepest human questionings that faith itself becomes
something real and relevant—and not some kind of restric-
tive system of religious rules.

To expand for just a moment on this last point—genuine faith is not some impersonal agreement with the truth
of a given set of religious beliefs. Real Christian faith is a
personal acceptance of Christ and of the way of life entailed
in being his disciple. And this way of life consists basically
in a set of developing relationships with other persons, relationships that (as indicated earlier) are truly "word of God"
for us. For that reason, what faith actually is can only be
learned as we try to live it out in the changing situations of
our days and years. For each of us faith is a somewhat
distinctive reality, conditioned by our particular personality and circumstances, even though we all believe in the
same God who is the Father of our Lord, Jesus Christ.
Christian faith is the responsible acceptance of life; it can
only be understood for what it is in the experience of
accepting life.

The Home as Privileged Place of Celebration

Which brings us to the topic of the home as *the* location of celebration, and therefore of Christian liturgy. Let us begin by making a proposal that in many ways is basic to everything we wish to say: For a long time, it has been taken for granted that a church (or its equivalent) was the ordinary place for liturgy and the home was the exceptional place; only on rare occasions, and for most people never, was the home the scene of a liturgical celebration. What we propose is that this is backwards; it is the home that should be the ordinary, the regular, situation of liturgical worship; the church should be the special and less ordinary place of liturgy. Now, this proposal is made, not to suggest that there should be a diminishing of good liturgy in churches, but in the hope that the home be rediscovered as the normal and basic location of liturgies which themselves would then feed into the larger group liturgy in the church.

But what would it mean to have liturgies regularly in the home, celebrated by a family or a group of families? Basically what it would mean is that Christians in family groupings would be celebrating the gift of life, the gift of one another, the gift of experiencing life happily because of the Christian faith that allowed them to see God as gracious and loving. To make this more concrete, let us try to describe it in terms of something that is being much discussed today—in sociology and psychology, in anthropology and the study of literature, in aesthetics and the study of religion: the *rhythms* that we all encounter in our lives.

To some extent, at least, we are only now becoming *explicitly* aware of these rhythms and of the profound way in which they influence us. We know that so-called "primitive" peoples were very much conditioned by the rhythms of nature: the rhythm of the seasons and the sequence of light and darkness, of planting and tending crops and harvest; but we had supposed that in our modern world with its movement away from the countryside and into cities with their mechanized way of life we were no longer deeply influenced by life rhythms. Now we are coming to know better. The patterns of rhythm may be changed, but we are just as deeply in tune or out of tune with life rhythms; and as a consequence we are happy or unhappy, peaceful or agitated, productive or frustrated. In an earlier and simpler age the rhythmic celebration of the Church's liturgical year took account of this need; but is liturgy capable of playing this role today?

There clearly is some basic rhythm in each person's individual growth and development, the rhythm of moving from birth through childhood into adolescence and then adulthood; but this can be very different from one instance to another, because of the particular culture and social situation and historical circumstances in which a person goes through these various "passages." For one person, blessed by a happy home and natural talents and plentiful vocational opportunities, the rhythms of personal development may be quite smooth and calm; for another person, problems and barriers may make the rhythm broken and jarring—scarcely a rhythm at all.

In this process of growth, in which bodily development and the evolution of consciousness are intertwined (as, for example, they are in the paradigm instance of entry into puberty, when the bodily changes have such far-reaching impact on the young adolescent's awareness of his or her own affective life), the family has a unique opportunity to make the various "passages" a joyful and productive rather than a frightening and painful experience.

People need to learn that it is good to be bodily, for it is our bodily dimension that allows us to function in space and time; the bodily aspect of our being makes beauty perceptible, makes consciousness itself possible; contrary to some beliefs, we can be truly spiritual and personal in proportion as we are more sensitively bodily.

Much of this growth in appreciation of our bodily being can be achieved by celebrating—birthdays, first day at school, graduation, successes of various kinds (like good report cards) that mark stages of achievement, coming to adulthood, or for that matter passing into middle or old age. And celebrating means a party of some kind, with singing and good food and dancing together—which obviously introduces us into the realm of ritual, even liturgical ritual, which from time immemorial has involved liturgical dance and ritual meals and hymns and psalms. Most probably such home celebrations would not be looked on as liturgy, which is just as well, because it would falsify them as ritual to introduce "liturgical elements" from outside into the natural celebration. All that would be needed to make them truly *Christian* liturgy would be a sense that families could celebrate in this way because they were blessed by this God who is the Father of Jesus Christ.

And in between such more obvious celebrations, there would be all those moments of experiencing music and beautiful objects and being grateful for them, the gradual (though partially frustrating) achieving of intellectual or creative skills, and the joy of having learned or having made something, and the conversations that help explain what is happening in one's life and that prepare for the next stage in the life rhythm. All these quiet moments of discovery and gratitude for life are part of creating that positive and thanks-giving attitude toward reality which is the foundation of all worship.

It is not only with the rhythms of personal development that we have to find resonance; the very rhythms of each individual are intertwined with the rhythms of our relationships to one another in human society. There is a certain patterned activity, a certain rhythm of doing things, that characterizes each group of people—be it a family, a nation, a neighborhood, or just a friendship between two persons. And each of these is distinct and somewhat different. The rhythms of life in a large city of today are quite different from the rhythms of a small Midwestern town in the early part of the century. Each friendship has its own rate and mode of growth; and one violates these rhythms at the risk of destroying the relationship.

Learning how to discern and then accept and then foster these inter-personal rhythms is delicate and difficult. What makes it even more difficult is the fact that we do not wish to agree with all the life rhythms of the world of humans around us. We may not wish to identify with the mad helter-skelter of acquisitiveness that is the rhythm of so many people's activity today. We may not wish to make the rhythm of headlong chasing after distractions our own life rhythm; we may wish to follow another drummer. Again, the family seems the ideal place to celebrate the genuine rhythms of relationship between persons, and in celebrating to become sensitive to the rhythms of human society.

To be bodily with others in such a way that bodiliness is a noble human endowment, a source of dignity and enrichment, to learn to accept one's own body with joy and frank wonder, and to reverence with open acceptance the

bodies of others—whether beautifully healthy or crip-
pled—this is a heritage that children claim from healthy
family life. And with this to develop with easy integrity a
sexual identity that can put one at ease in one's dealings
with others, that can give one a secure location in the world
of men and women. But for this to happen, parents must in
candor and maturity celebrate their relationship to one
another as man and woman, and celebrate with each of
their children his or her emerging sexuality. More than this,
it is in the family that persons can make together the critical
discovery that the fundamental rhythms of their relationships to one another are deeply personal without being sexual—a discovery that hopefully can be carried on in a
Christian life that honors the Pauline principle that in the
Body of Christ there are no dividing distinctions between
master and servant, between male and female.

It is in the family, as nowhere else, that persons can
(though it takes effort and love to do it!) learn to live the
rhythms of agreement and disagreement, conflict and
reconciliation, admiration and disillusionment, honesty
and deceit, love and infidelity; and it is these rhythms that
must be accepted as the human condition, accepted by the
family as a community as it celebrates its being a community despite the threats to unity implicit in these changing
patterns of personal life. To put it another way: What
families are meant to discover and to live out as they
celebrate together is that they are forgiving and forgiven
lovers of one another. To know this is to be mature; to rejoice in this is to celebrate the presence of the Spirit of God.

Explicit celebrations are critically important in this
process: A birthday can be the occasion for letting the individual know how the rest of the family rejoices in his or
her being and being for them; a special party can cement a

reconciliation that ends a conflict between certain members of the family; celebration of an engagement or of a marriage can make it clear that the family is opening up its inner circle of love to a new member; parties given for friends of the family can celebrate the value that the family places on human friendships, and the character of those parties can voice the kind of joyous respect the members of the family have for other persons; and Christian families can learn to celebrate the sending forth of a member of the family "on mission"—whether it be to begin a higher education preparing for some life of service in the world, or to engage in some work that hopefully will bring a better life to some of the world's disadvantaged, or even to undertake some specific and short-range project. Perhaps we should regain the early Christians' sense of hospitality and their sense of sending forth from such familial gatherings apostles to preach the "good news."

Our specific set of interpersonal relationships, with its constantly evolving rhythms, is part of the yet more vast rhythms of the created cosmos and the centuries-long rhythms of human history. To these also we humans must learn to become attuned, so that we are creative and not disruptive, so that we are agents for the true growth of humanity which can only take place in harmony and peace. But these larger rhythms are precisely those that engage us in the day-by-day course of experience—the rhythm of light and darkness, the rhythm of good and nurture and health and sickness, the rhythm of life and death, the rhythm of sameness and change, the rhythmic activity of all those elemental forces of nature that so constantly influence our lives. We have learned in these last few years how carefully we must respect these rhythms, at the peril of our sanity and our health, at the peril of our very endurance as a race.

There is an instinctive wisdom in the human race that has always had some insight into the radical importance of these cosmic rhythms. Every folk religion paid tribute to them in seasonal festivals and magical ritual. Rejecting the magic, both Israel and Christianity absorbed into their own liturgies much of these old "pagan" rites and symbols. The Christian liturgical cycle is itself the most detailed example of ritual respect for the rhythms of creation. In our day there is a great need to recapture (at least the spirit of) the ways in which various ethnic groups observed this liturgical cycle through simple home rituals and then carried their observances over into their congregational celebrations of the chief liturgical feasts.

However, Christianity has always believed that there is one ultimate and governing rhythm that is the "secret" to all else: the rhythm of "the kingdom of God." When one uses this term, one is referring to God's *rule,* to his providential guidance of all that is and particularly of the affairs of humankind. God's creative and redeeming activity has its own rhythms (some people would prefer to call them "laws"), its own patterns of leading humans freely to their destiny. It is an activity that works through God's own Word and Spirit, an activity that is revealed in the history of Jesus Christ. It is an activity that continues to be manifest in the lives of men and women in our world today.

The rhythms of the kingdom of God are the rhythms of promise and fulfillment, of God's call and human response, of human sin and God's merciful redemption, of new life coming to be through death, of self-giving that leads to final self-realization (even for God!). These rhythms, made explicit for us in Scripture and Christian tradition, are not foreign to nor even apart from the other life rhythms of which we have spoken; rather, they run as a dominant leit-motiv through the complicated harmonics of the other rhythms, giving them basic pattern but also distinguishing the harmonious from the dissonant.

But because the rhythms of God's kingdom are the rhythms of his Spirit in our midst, they can be discerned only by living them; the Spirit of God cannot ultimately be explained, but only experienced—and experienced in every mode of our human life. So again we come to the family's indispensable role: If we Christians are to perceive the rhythms of God's guidance and respond to them in freedom, our homes must become communities in which the presence of God's Spirit is celebrated. This will not be something added to what we have already described; it will not be extra celebration added to the natural celebrations of family life; rather, it will be the final dimension of all these others.

In any family festivity, the presence of a dear friend of the family adds a special something to the celebration. In somewhat similar fashion, all the celebrations of a Chris-tian family have an added element because of the presence of the risen Christ in his Spirit. This occurs, of course, only in proportion as the family believes in the reality of the risen Jesus; and one of the principal purposes of liturgical celebrations in the home is to keep the family members aware of this presence of Christ. Unfortunately, in the past this was somewhat obscured by the belief that the risen Jesus was "up in heaven" and was present on earth only in the reserved Eucharist in our churches. But with the recovered awareness that the "resurrection" of Jesus means his constant presence to all of us who believe in him, we can without pseudo-theological barriers regain a deepened consciousness of his abiding presence in our lives. As members of a family do grow in this awareness, family life gradually becomes a continuing liturgy, a constant profession of faith—which is what Christian faith is all about.

The past few decades have offered to us Christians unprecedented opportunity to revitalize our liturgical worship, and great strides have indeed been taken. Yet there remains for us an exciting but somewhat frightening task—frightening because of the radical and large-scale evolution that must take place. Revision of liturgical forms has made and will make a major contribution. Greater freedom on the part of local communities to formulate appropriate liturgies will be of immense help. But ultimately the creation of a Christian liturgical worship that is truly human, truly a sacrament of the indwelling presence of the risen Christ, truly a word of revelation and therefore a challenge to conversion, will spring from the understanding of men and women regarding their identity as Christians. Any genuine liturgical advance in the years ahead will rest upon the education of this understanding and upon the art of translating this understanding into appropriate celebration. Only if the Christian family becomes the teacher of celebration will larger Christian communities know how to worship the Father of our Lord Jesus Christ, by gathering together to celebrate the rhythms of his saving love.

For Further Reading

Cooke, Bernard. *Ministry to Word and Sacraments*. Philadelphia: Fortress Press, 1976.

The Family as a Center of Ministry

by Marie and Brennan Hill

Marie and Brennan Hill are both involved in religious education. Marie is the director of religious education in St. Matthew's Parish in Voorheesville, New York, and Brennan is the director of parish programs for the diocese of Albany, New York. Both have published several books and numerous articles on adult catechesis.

In this essay the Hills explain how a family of vibrant faith can practice a true ministry in the fields of catechesis, liturgy, and social justice.

In the 1980s the Church is increasingly recognizing the family as the very foundation of the Church's life and as a largely untapped source of ministry. Marriage is no longer viewed as a secondary state of life but as a vocation in its own right, and the family is recognized as a primordial church community.

The gradual deterioration of family life and the ensuing alarming effects nationally and locally have made us realize the importance of family life. If the family is in trouble, then both society and the Church face a crisis. The only possible response is a return to our foundations and an all-out effort to nurture and support families.

For too long the Church thought it could bypass the family. Clergy and members of religious congregations were often cut off from domestic life in a monastic system of education and spirituality that separated them from a basic life source and set them over and against the very people they were to serve. Great emphasis was placed on the religious formation of those "with a vocation," while the sacramentality of marriage was neglected. Lay people were offered inadequate formation in appropriate spirituality, and little opportunity to exercise ministry.

The parochial school system also represented a circumvention of the family. Sisters were given the awesome responsibility of building the faith of children. An attitude of "Let Sister do it" crept in, and many parents gradually unburdened themselves of the responsibility to form the religious life of children within the home. We visit many parishes where the school has been closed and the sisters have been long gone, yet parents still sit back waiting for someone to show up and take on the faith formation of their children.

But in recent years parish religious education programs have revealed the importance of the family, for it has become obvious that catechists can only supplement what goes on at home. Parents *are* the primary religious educators. We have said it often, but only now are we beginning to believe it. As a result, many parishes are actually giving parent and adult formation priority over that of child education, while others are turning to total family programs.

This new emphasis on the importance of the family comes at the same time when there is a great deal of discussion about a crisis in ministry. The former system of expecting a small minority of Catholics (priests, brothers, and sisters) to carry all the responsibilities of ministry while the vast majority remain passive simply won't work anymore. The decline in numbers of candidates for these vocations, as well as the tremendous complexity of pastoral demands, signals the need for a radically different approach to ministry.

It is our conviction that the family can indeed be a novitiate for ministerial formation, and a unique and rich resource for service. After discussing how the family is indeed the epitome of what Church is, we will suggest an appropriate theology of ministry and then point out concrete areas in which ministry can be exercised in families: catechesis, liturgy, and social justice.

The Family as Church

Since Vatican II the Church's consciousness of itself has expanded immensely. The documents of the Council go far beyond the post-Reformation notion that the Church is exclusively identified with Catholicism. The Church is instead identified with people and thus ranges from the entire human community to the smallest and most intimate community, the family. Rooted in the mystery of God's presence, the Church is somehow expressed in all religious communities, but uniquely in families.

The Church now recognizes the family as the basic unit in both society and religion. It is, therefore, genuinely Church. As the revolutionary statement in *Lumen Gentium* (n. 11) puts it, "The family is the domestic Church." And Karl Rahner reminds us that such a description of the family is not a simile. We are not saying that the family is *like* the Church or that it is *part* of the Church. The family *is* the Church in that it is a genuinely ecclesial expression of God's presence among specific communities of people. The family is in fact a local church, and local churches are not merely members of the total Church. They are actual realizations of what the Church is as a whole.[1]

If the family is the Church in miniature, then it has within itself the essential aspects of Church and can be an authentic ecclesial experience for family members. What are those essential aspects of Church?

Primary in the Church's life is the experience of *sharing the presence of Jesus*. Now the experience of unconditional love between spouses and among parents and children who accept one another as they are is a true taste of love which speaks of the presence of the Lord. The compassion and forgiveness of Jesus is shown forth by an abused child's forgiving a parent. The fidelity of the risen Lord to the dying is mirrored as we share the death of a loved one. This latter point was brought home to us recently in a letter from a friend of ours who had lost his five-year-old son. He told us that the youngster was able to communicate with his parents until the very end, and that the death was an experience of the Lord's presence in their family. The father ended his letter by saying, "We're glad our little one shared his life and his death with us." What some would consider to be a tragic annihilation of a young life was actually an experience of Church—Jesus' presence among his people. And of course true resurrection shines out as family members recover from an illness, find employment after a long time out of work, or solve a difficult problem.

Besides the consciousness of Jesus' presence, another aspect of Church is *community*. The Church is people in fellowship with Jesus and with one another. Now, no other community offers the intimacy of relationship that the family does. There is a closeness here that can form and open and nourish the potential of the person and that can, on the other hand, harm and even destroy the person. Like the whole Church, the family is a community of diverse personalities with powers to create and powers to destroy. The very struggle of diverse individuals trying to overcome their weaknesses and achieve unity is indeed a localized experience of what is going on in the larger Church community.

Families, therefore, experience Church in the precious moments of affection and celebration as well as in the tense moments, stressful situations, and even broken relationships. The Church is not an ideal community, and neither is the family. Both experience deep divisions and hostilities as well as ecstatic times of closeness and unity. At such a critical time of breakup in our family structures, the family reveals itself even more authentically as Church and underlines the need for constant renewal and healing.

The Church, both universal and local, is a *sacramental community*. As such, it celebrates the presence of Jesus in its midst in symbolic fashion. In Baptism, new members have their lives immersed in the very life of Jesus, and the Church family pledges to nourish this life. In Eucharist, families celebrate their effort to maintain their fragile unity with the Lord and with one another. In Reconciliation, they celebrate their commitment to conversion from selfishness, their ongoing effort to forgive the hurts and wounds they inflict on each other.

The family, like the whole Church, is a sacramental community in its own right, in that it has within itself the power to be a dynamic symbol both to its own members and to those around them. We have many examples of this in our own neighborhood: the family who adopted a girl, and though time after time rejected by her, always welcomed her back; the family who took in the baby of a mother who had a breakdown, allowing the mother time to recover; the divorced mother who struggled so hard to give a loving family experience to her children and who always opened her home to those in need; the widow who became the local grandmother to all the children in the block, offering them her tenderness and her wisdom.

The family, like the Church, is a *servant community*. Domestic life requires much self-sacrifice, hard work, and sensitivity to the needs of others. Parents of small children often live a spartan life of limited sleep, tremendous stress, and many demands upon them. Parents of teenagers especially find a great deal expected of them, with often little gratitude in return. The need for patient listening and love, even in the face of apparent rejection, presents great difficulties. Yet even with these serious responsibilities, many parents find time to serve the larger community. We think of a certain father of a large family who still finds time to work with retarded children on weekends. We

know a number of teenagers who are actively involved in
the primary religious education classes in their parish.
Many families in our parish are truly ministerial, truly a
servant community, in their immediate response to anyone
in need. In many of these instances, individuals and
families are bringing home to others the realization that being Church means serving.

The family, then, is a vital and dynamic expression of
the local Church. As such, it experiences the saving
presence of Jesus, struggles to be a community of love that is
both sacrament and servant, and therefore rightfully shares
in the mission of the Church to minister in Christ's name.

A Theology of Ministry

A radically different theology of ministry is slowly emerging which enables families to assume their proper role in the
mission of the Church. This theology, which is based on
biblical foundations, challenges the vertical clerical system
of ministry and opens ministry to all those who have been
baptized into the life of Jesus.

Clerical notions of ministry still seem to prevail in today's Church. A distinct class system exists wherein many
bishops and priests continue to think that the work of the
Church is theirs exclusively. In this hierarchical or vertical
model, the vast majority of Catholics see themselves as recipients of rather than as initiators of pastoral work. Lay
ministry is still at best supplemental and is often carried out
not so much out of a sense of personal gift and calling as
through permission or benign commissioning.

Although there are many hopeful signs that all this is
changing, there are also signals of retrenchment. Some

seminaries are still training a clerical elite who seem to oppose the populist movement in the Church. Moreover, women who have excellent gifts and training for ministry are finding it difficult to find positions. The permanent deacon program often continues to be modeled after the seminary system and usually fails to offer clear identity to its candidates. The liturgical ministries are officially closed to women, and their initiation in parishes at times is resisted by both clergy and laity. What is more astonishing, even the official ministry of catechist excludes women and therefore must be unofficially assumed (mostly by women).

The messages from Rome are not encouraging. Pope Paul II's decision to impede if not stop the dispensation process makes it all but impossible for priests to leave the active priesthood and continue ministry. Moreover, his Easter message of 1979 to priests reiterated the essential difference between the ordained priesthood and the priesthood of the laity. Celibacy was described as necessary if priesthood is to be "for others." Marriage was dealt with once again in terms of procreation and of the man taking care of wife and children. Certainly no ground was broken here for new models of ministry or for recognizing the ministerial possibilities within families.

But concomitant with these indications of regression to the vertical, clerical style of ministry are signs of advances in *shared* ministry that challenge the old system. Many more laity are aware of their personal gifts and are quietly giving themselves to the work of the Lord. Pastoral teams consisting of a cross-section of laity, clergy, and members of religious orders are being formed in parishes. Some bishops and priests are sincerely calling forth others to share in the ministry of the Church.[2]

These advances herald a new theology of ministry, one which will restore to all Christians their birthright of doing the work of the Lord. It is a theology which makes it possible to see the family as a genuine center of ministry and a valuable source of service to the Church. It places emphasis on Jesus, Baptism, personal gifts received from the Holy Spirit, and a renewed sense of shared ministry.

This theology of ministry begins with a person, the person of *Jesus*. He is *the* minister and *the* priest. All ministry, be it ordained or unordained, official or unofficial, is an extension of the ministry of Jesus. As one biblical scholar put it, "Jesus concluded his ministry on earth by putting it into our hands. He sends us in the very same way and for the same purpose for which the Father sent him."[3] The risen Lord is the one who is ministering, and his Spirit moves where it wills. He is present in the world, teaching, healing, saving, through the instrumentality of *all* his disciples. He stands as both the model and power of ministry.

The basic title for ministry, then, is not an ecclesiastical office or position, although these specify ministries, but *Baptism*. Once a person has been plunged into the very life of Jesus in Baptism, that person shares in Jesus' ministry. This sacrament imparts both a right and a responsibility to use one's gifts to carry on the work of the Church. This was clearly brought out in Vatican II.

> These faithful are by Baptism made one body with Christ and are established among the people of God. They are, in their own way, made sharers in the priestly, prophetic, and kingly functions of Christ. They carry out their own part in the mission of the whole Christian people with respect to the Church and the world.[4]

An appreciation of *the gifts of the Spirit* is also basic in this renewed theology of ministry. Until recently, the Roman Catholic tradition had all but lost its understanding of the presence of the Spirit of the Lord and the giftedness that such presence brings to all persons. The Spirit was largely thought of as confined to the magisterium, and gifts for ministry were narrowly limited to Orders. Now we are experiencing an amazing new consciousness of the Spirit of the Lord. Catholics are much more aware of how the Spirit directs their lives and gives them unique and enduring gifts for serving others. Those who in the past offered occasional services out of a sense of Christian duty are now more aware of a more stable and formal participation in ministry.

The evolution to *a broader notion of ministry* includes a reexamination of offices in the Church. Originally, these offices (of bishop, priest, deacon) were developed in the community so that individuals could officially exercise their gifts and, as leaders, nurture the gifts of others with whom they shared ministry. Unfortunately, the offices gradually monopolized ministry, and the word *ministerium* was applied only to the activity of the ordained. Even Vatican II, in the midst of all its efforts to renew ministry, kept the old terminology.[5]

In an age of shared ministry, our bishops and priests will have to see their pastoral leadership in terms of enabling and facilitating. It will be their task to make the laity aware of their personal gifts, to nurture these gifts, and to give lay persons real opportunities to exercise their rights and responsibilities in ministry.

We suggest that the thrust of this new thinking be directed to families. It is here, in this most basic community of the Church, that people can best be brought to an awareness of the role they can play in carrying out the work of the Lord. We think that such a step will not only provide a much-needed strengthening of families but will provide the Church as a whole with resources for ministry in today's society.

Now that we have shown that the family is an authentic local Church with a rightful share in the Church's ministry and have explored an appropriate theology of ministry, we want to examine three specific areas wherein ministry occurs within families that are effectively preparing family members to serve the larger community.

The Ministry of Catechesis

Catechesis is one of the foremost ministries carried on within the family. The root meaning of the word *catechesis* is "to echo," and the family is the place where the first echoes of Jesus' message should be heard. The home is the ideal environment for nourishing faith and bringing it to maturity. Religious educators have long ago concluded that instructing children without at the same time attending to parental involvement produces minimal effects. Thus the current interest in total family programs and in-depth parent sessions.

By catechesis, then, we do not mean the traditional formal instruction, but the process whereby family members nurture one another's faith. We have scared many parents off by telling them that they are the "primary religious educators" yet not adequately explaining what this means. Some feel that this is merely the parish saying, "We don't know what to do, so you do it." Others panic at the thought that they now are expected to be qualified teachers who will formally instruct their children. What should be clarified is that parents nurture the faith more through living and sharing than through formal instruction. The depth of their own faith commitment and the level of their own understanding of the faith are the factors which most affect other family members. Father Bernard Häring, in recounting his days as a medic in the German Army in World War II, says that the deepest faith he ever found was in Polish peasant families who had little or no formal education. For them the faith was a lived experience, integral to their daily activities.[6]

We should make families more aware that much of what they consider everyday living is in fact genuine ministry and catechesis. For instance, parents should know that their unconditional personal acceptance of their children is all-important and is integrally linked to catechesis. Dr. Urie Bronfenbrenner tells us that every child needs someone who is completely "crazy" about him or her.[7] Children sense very early how much they are loved and what conditions, if any, are placed on that love. Those who never experience unconditional love in the home will find it hard for the rest of their lives to love themselves or love others in a healthy fashion since, as Abraham Maslow tells us, mature love is an overflow of genuine self-esteem. Needless to say, it is difficult for a person with a poor self-image to accept the unconditional love of God. So the daily struggle of parents to love their children must be viewed as fundamental to any real catechesis.

Faith maturity also hinges on the way family members care for one another during the inevitable conflicts and crises in family life. We have grown close to a neighbor whose sixteen children range from thirty to three. She is so deeply and warmly faithful in the midst of extreme difficulty that she has been an inspiration to her family and to many others. She is convinced that the "Man upstairs" will always stand by her, and this conviction has rubbed off on her children. Together they have overcome untold hardships. The faith of another family we know has been greatly strengthened by the death of the mother. She lingered bravely with cancer, often crying because she had to give up the care of her husband and children. Her final acknowledgment that God would take care of them not only enabled her to let go peacefully; it also continues to sustain the faith of her family.

The teenage years are usually stressful times for families, and the way families handle adolescent conflicts leaves indelible marks on the whole family psyche, including its faith life. "Having a teenager" can be the source of marital problems, alcoholism, and alienation. It is difficult and sometimes impossible for parents to accept, enjoy, or even like their teenager during those years. And the young people often complain that their parents are too authoritarian, old-fashioned, or lacking in understanding. Much of this conflict spills over into religious areas, with arguments about going to church and the morality of drinking and premarital sex. Parents who can remember the turmoil of their own adolescence and patiently get in touch with the feelings of the children perform a service that is crucial to the family's faith life. In our discussions with parents we have discovered that adults always look back with admiration on parents who "hung in" with them during the stormy times and allowed them the freedom to grow and make independent decisions. They recall with fondness those parents who invited and encouraged them in areas of faith instead of using force or threats.

Conversely, teens need to be made aware of the effects their religious attitudes can have on the faith of their parents. The adolescents' struggle with faith does not give them license to tread crassly on what their parents hold sacred or to scoff at cherished religious practices. The young, like all of us, have the power to nurture the faith of others as well as the power to weaken or even destroy faith.

We often do not realize how the young can enliven the faith of the whole community. We are often so preoccupied with lamenting that our young don't want to go to church or religion class that we don't see that many young people are serious about the faith and can serve as an inspiration to young and old alike. Yet some Protestant communities do effectively put their youth in the forefront as examples of freshness and vitality. Oral Roberts and Rex Humbard often feature their younger family members and other young people as key evangelizers. We could well learn a lesson from this approach. If our dedicated young people were given center stage at times, they would offer hope to older Church members and affect their own peers and younger children as well. We seem to be unaware that the Spirit could gift our young people with the power to proclaim the Gospel and to witness to Christian living.

The Church's revision of the sacraments has had a great effect on the catechetical process within families. Baptisms, which were once isolated services on Sunday afternoon, are now becoming significant family events. Baptisms provide occasions for parents to broaden their religious understanding and to attend to their own faith life. Godparents are now selected with much more of an eye to their giving Christian witness. The ceremony itself, especially when celebrated at home, makes a deep impact not only on the immediate family but also on friends and relatives.

Parental involvement in the sacramental preparation

of children has made a major impact on families. Not only does it reveal to the children that parents take these sacramental events seriously, but it also comes as a special grace to parents. One parent recently told us that it was his little daughter's First Communion that straightened out his life and brought him back to the Church. He had lost touch with the faith, was drinking too much, and was overwhelmed by pressures at work. His daughter's enthusiasm for receiving the Lord reenkindled his own love for Jesus and moved him to take his religion seriously. And we have often witnessed instances where parents finally realized the implications of their baptismal vows when a youngster in the family was confirmed. These are clear instances where a lively catechetical ministry is going on in the family context.

We have found that emphasizing the family in sacramental celebration can be a way to welcome families who perhaps at other times felt excluded. For instance, at the time of First Communion our parish always stresses that "family" means those who want to share this special event with the child. Single parents and the divorced, as well as relatives and friends of the child, are invited to participate in the event. Frequently this becomes a living illustration of Christian reconciliaton. Single parents, who often struggle heroically to maintain a genuine family, no longer find themselves labeled as parents of "broken homes." Those in irregular marriages are made to feel that they are welcomed and loved. Often older brothers and sisters who have felt cut off take this as an invitation to rejoin the community.

The strengthening of catechesis within families has been instrumental in bringing forth many who now feel called to extend this ministry beyond the limits of their own families. The ministry of the catechist is one of the most exciting within the Church today. Adults of all ages, and teens as well, are coming forth willing to share their faith with others. A task which used to be looked at as doing a favor for the pastor or helping Sister is now becoming a full-blown ministry. These "co-workers of the priestly order" are emerging as our best informed and most faith-filled people in the community.[8] Here families have become a major resource for a ministry which is at the very heart of the Christian life.

Liturgical Ministry

The dichotomy between everyday life and liturgy is gradually breaking down. Catholics are becoming increasingly aware that liturgy is not an isolated event in church but an ongoing process of prayer and worship which finds its roots in the family and culminates in public communal celebrations. There is a demand for a spirituality designed for domestic life, and at the same time there is growing impatience with dull and routine Masses which neither sustain families nor have relevance to everyday life. As a result, many families are engaging in a true liturgical ministry as they integrate prayer and worship into the home life and seek out parishes where the family can be nourished and strengthened in an atmosphere of warmth and friendliness.

One vital liturgical area in which family members can minister to one another is that of prayer. So many of the traditional forms of prayer have been set aside that we all find ourselves somewhat adrift. We recently asked advice on this from an expert in spirituality. He recommended that family members spend some of their quieter moments placing themselves in the presence of the Lord. He said that once we build this openness to the Spirit into our everyday experience, we will reestablish prayer in our lives. "Otherwise," he said, "something dies inside of us." He observed that waiting until we have an hour or so for prayer is usually unrealistic for the busy parent or youngster, but that placing ourselves in God's presence takes but a few moments and can be immensely refreshing.

Sometimes it is our children who help us to appreciate the value of prayer. After a hectic meal preparation, our family often sits down and begins, only to be stopped by our three-year-old who wants us to join hands and "thank God for supper." At other times, sharing our children's wonder at the first sight of the ocean or their awe at caterpillars and stars can create a prayerful atmosphere by bringing us into a sharper awareness of God's presence. We have also been impressed by the discipline with which our young ones practice Yoga and T.M. This has made us more comfortable with openly admitting to others that we need a definite time for meditation.

The ministry of the Word is also gaining ground among families, and the Scriptures are beginning to find their way back into many Christian homes. For one reason or another, many of us have not been comfortable with the Bible, and so it has not been the source of nourishment it could be for families. Now some families read from the Scripture before meals or before a journey. Friends of ours gather the family one hour a week, have an appropriate reading from the Bible, and then discuss what is happening in the family. Gradually our families are beginning to open themselves to the immense power of the Word and are experiencing the Lord's presence in this special way.

Celebration is another vital part of Christian life, and

the family community has many opportunities to share in this area. Celebrations are commonplace among families, particularly for birthdays, Thanksgiving, Christmas, and Easter. Careful preparation and emphasis on the faith dimension of these occasions pay huge dividends in closeness, communication, and enjoyment. In addition, the natural anticipation and enthusiasm for these occasions becomes linked with religion and prepares family members for lively participation in the parish celebration of liturgical feasts.

Celebration of the sacraments has much more meaning for those have experienced the essence of these sacraments at home. One hassled mother told of how her family came to realize the meaning of Reconciliation. One rainy day while her husband was away, she was at her wits' end because of the noise, arguments, and disrespect from her five children. As they gathered at the table for supper she rather self-righteously announced that each one should ask forgiveness for the hurts inflicted on the family that day. She was really touched as each one, including the three-year-old, confessed and asked for forgiveness. Then the five-year-old said, "Your turn, Mom." She, too, had to confess how she had contributed to the hurt. When she finished, they all laughed together and peace was restored. There was no need for lengthy theological explanations about the sacrament of Reconciliation after that.

Another family in our parish cared for a grandmother dying with cancer for over a year. Like their parents, the four children, aged ten to eighteen, all experienced the emotions of denial, anger, disgust, and impatience, but they anointed the old woman daily with their care, visits, and love, and learned what it meant to minister to the dying.

Conscientious liturgical formation and ministry at home spills over into parish life. The ministry that family members offer one another in prayer, Scripture reading, and celebration provides the base for an active partaking in public worship. In this sense parish liturgy is family centered, not in the limited meaning of mother-father-children attending Mass,, but in the sense that family ties and experiences provide the chemistry for good liturgy. A church full of people who have a feeling for community and who are accustomed to ministering to others in prayer and God's Word and worship at home are well prepared for a shared Eucharist. One senses this particularly at children's liturgies. The atmosphere is usually relaxed, people are more inclined to smile, and the whole experience is more intelligible than usual. Especially at moments when little ones recite, perform tasks, or sing, the reaction of all reveals that family bonds and family experience are perhaps the strongest force uniting parish communities and giving all a feeling for ministering to one another.

Formation in prayer and the Word and worship at home also overflows into parish life in the exercise of the liturgical ministries. The notion that lay people are unworthy to proclaim the Scriptures, distribute the Eucharist, or lead in song is breaking down, particularly among those who have become comfortable with liturgy at home. Many more people, both young and old, are coming forward, not so much out of duty to help Father, but because they are conscious of a call to exercise genuine ministry. As both the clergy and congregations accustom themselves to this phenomenon, the old divisions between clergy and laity are breaking down and the way is being opened for shared ministry.

The home and parish complement each other in

liturgical renewal. The more families grow in prayer and the Word and worship, the more people are coming forth to serve communal worship. By the same token, vital and warmly shared parish liturgy is deeply affecting both spirituality and ministry in the family.

The Ministry of Social Justice

The ultimate goal of catechesis and liturgy is to move Christians to care for and serve others. Since Vatican II, the Church has translated this loving service into a commitment to transform the world. The international synod of Roman Catholic bishops in 1971 went so far as to say that social justice is constitutive of the Church's mission.[9] In other words, ministry on all levels of the Church, from the universal to the domestic, is lacking an essential unless it struggles to liberate the oppressed from social sin.

The family, then, has no other alternative but to be concerned about the rights and needs of others on international and local levels. Persistent threats to environment, the menacing arms race, problems of worldwide hunger, the tremendous imbalance in the use of goods and energy by Americans, and the violation of human rights are not mere political issues. They strike at the heart of human dignity and have to be addressed by anyone attempting to share the Lord's ministry. The inequity in this country, which allots the top 20% of American families over 40% of all family income and 60% of the nation's wealth, leaving the bottom 20% with less than 6% of all family income and little or no assets, must be of major concern to anyone attempting to live the Gospel life.[10]

Unfortunately, many families are so caught up in the tensions of our economy that they have little time for the less fortunate. Consumerism is fast becoming a chronic family malady, and even tiny tots become fledgling consumers as they watch television. Parents and young ones alike often find themselves so job-oriented that they have little time for anything but work and a minimum of recreation. The shopping malls have gradually become the social centers in our communities, and whole families spend large amounts of their free time chasing down sales and seeking a kind of "buying therapy." Add an energy crunch to all this frenetic activity to cope with the economy, and it is not too difficult to understand why a mood of quiet desperation is settling into families and into the nation as a whole. Such a situation hardly leaves room for much concern for those who are really most in need, the poor and deprived of our society.

Still, in the midst of all this an increasing number of families are striving for simplicity and are interested in sharing their personal wealth with others. Simplicity, as the Shakers lived it, meant "not too much and not too little." For many families, such simplicity means smaller cars and homes, use of alternate sources of energy such as wood and sun, refusal to succumb to advertising, minimal if any TV watching, simple dress, food, and drink, and an active involvement in social justice issues such as hunger, poverty, and disarmament.

Returning to simple living so that one can serve others requires heroic effort on the part of all the family members. It is here that we enter a unique kind of ministry. By assisting and supporting one another in the discipline of simplicity, family members free one another to share money and time with the disenfranchised of the larger community. In our society it is not easy for children to accustom themselves to having less than their friends do. Neither is it easy for young ones to resist badgering their parents for all the things which society and neighbors feel everyone must own. Such an attitude requires a certain toughness and independence in children, and forming such attitudes calls for a great deal of patience and understanding from parents. At the same time, parents find it difficult to discipline their own innate desire to acquire things and to deal with the natural pride that drives them to be equal to if not better off than neighbors. Society often interprets simple living as failure or lack of initiative. Families committed to a simple way of life will often get the distinct sensation that they are trying to swim against the current. Achieving this posture, therefore, requires great mutual support and much open communication.

Simple living is not an end in itself. Its purpose is to provide families with the inner freedom and the resources to reach out to those in need. As families achieve a simple life-style, they are able to open their lives and homes to others and "let go" of the surplus money and goods which simplicity provides. Such sharing is a genuine ministry within a Church newly concerned with the transformation of society.

We have witnessed many such families who conduct a kind of ministry that can be best done in a home environment. Taking an unwed mother into a family during her time of need can provide an atmosphere and care seldom duplicated by an institution. Opening one's home to youngsters and teens who have poor situations in their own homes offers an experience of acceptance and love upon which they can build their lives. Assisting and counseling persons going through a separation or divorce can provide them with the support they need at such a tragic time. And there are many other such crisis situations which can be best responded to by the family unit.

We have also seen the economic power which families who live simply can exert. In our own area a number of families were able to provide comfortable housing for a family that had lived in a broken-down shack for years. Because they were families, they were able to do this sensitively and in such a way that the needy persons didn't feel they were getting a handout or losing their dignity.

There is great corporate power in families bound together and seeking social justice. It is a power often better recognized by big business than by the families themselves. Cesar Chavez stressed many times during his lettuce boycott that his struggle for the rights of migrant workers was made possible because many families offered him strong support. The movements against violence on television, promotion of junk food, sexual exploitation in advertising, or the use of nuclear power make progress only when families organize and insist on their rights. Families are in the ideal situation to pressure the media and big business into forming a social conscience. A great bonus from such common effort and ministry comes in the form of stronger family bonds.

To sum up, the current Church emphasis on the family opens tremendous possibilities for ministry. The family is indeed a valid expression of the Church itself. Given the proper theology of ministry that is Christ-centered and open to shared ministry, the family can within itself exercise a true pastoral ministry. At the same time, the family can serve as an ideal training ground for ministry, particularly in the areas of catechesis, liturgy, and social justice.

Notes

1. Karl Rahner, *Studies in Modern Theology* (London: Herder, 1965), pp. 293-94.
2. See, for example, Bishop Howard Hubbard's pastoral letter, "We Are His People," Diocese of Albany, New York.
3. Stephen Doyle, O.F.M., "To Minister as Jesus Did," *St. Anthony Messenger*, March 1, 1979, pp. 15-19.
4. *Lumen Gentium*, n. 31.
5. "Ordained and Lay Ministry: Theological Update," *Crux* (newsletter), May 14, 1979.
6. Bernard Haring, *Embattled Witness* (New York: Seabury Press, 1976).
7. Urie Bronfenbrenner, "Nobody Home: The Erosion of the American Family," *Psychology Today*, May 1977, pp. 42-47.
8. *Ad Gentes*, n. 17.
9. J. Gremillion, ed., "Justice in the World," in *The Gospel of Peace and Justice* (Maryknoll, New York: Orbis, 1976), p. 514.
10. Kenneth Keniston, *All our Children: The American Family Under Pressure* (New York: Harcourt Brace Jovanovich, 1977), p. 26.

For Further Reading

Cooke, Bernard. *Ministry to Word and Sacraments.* Philadelphia: Fortress Press, 1976.

Hater, Robert J. *The Ministry Explosion.* Dubuque: Wm. C. Brown Co., 1979.

Haughton, Rosemary, "On Discovering Community." *Catholic Mind*, June 1979, pp. 49-57.

Kochtitzky, Robert, ed. *Alternative Celebrations Catalogue.* 4th ed. Bloomington, Ind.: Alternatives, 1978.

Taylor, John. *Enough Is Enough: A Biblical Call for Moderation in a Consumer-Oriented Society.* Minneapolis: Augsburg Publishing House, 1977.

Van Cauwelaert, J. "Ministry in Today's Christian Communities." *Living Light*, Spring 1973, pp. 119-27.

Family Learning Teams and Renewed Understanding of the Parish

by Mercedes and Joseph Iannone

The Iannones are co-directors of the National Training Center for Family Learning Teams. They have had experience in family religious education in many parishes over the past seven years. The Iannone family makes its home in Mt. Vernon, Virginia.

In this essay the authors describe the nature and purpose of family learning teams and suggest some ramifications which could flow from their implementation.

We believe that Family Learning Teams, a process-structure for family-centered catechesis, exemplify the renewed ecclesiology of Vatican II, best described in terms of "co-responsibility."

Our aim in this essay is to explore this new understanding of parish and of family-centered catechesis and to offer a design of local church which incorporates this twofold understanding. We will begin by describing "collegial subsidiarity" in practice as a desirable way of being Church. Secondly, we will explore how to use family-centered catechesis as the basic ecclesial component for implementing collegial subsidiarity at the grassroots of the Church. Finally, we will offer a model which grows out of a Family Learning Team catechetical structure and which concretizes collegial subsidiarity in practice.

By way of introduction it will be helpful to describe the terms *family*, *catechesis*, and *Family Learning Team* as we use them here.

Family in this context refers to any "household of faith." The household may consist of a single parent and children, a widow or widower living alone, a developing family, an "empty-nest" couple, or an extended family where three generations live together. Since fewer than half of the families we deal with are nuclear families with children, we must be aware that the term *family* as used here refers not just to nuclear families but to any "household of faith."

The second term which needs clarification is *catechesis*. Educating, teaching, and instructing are all parts of catechesis but are not the totality. The purpose of catechesis is to make a person's "faith become living, conscious, and active through the light of instruction" (*General Catechetical Directory*, n. 17, *National Catechetical*

Directory, n. 32) so "it does not do justice to catechesis to think of it as instruction alone" (*National Catechetical Directory,* n. 35). Sharing faith in community, nurturing a social conscience, and experiencing worship are as constitutive of the catechetical ministry of the Church as is teaching the message.

Finally a description of *Family Learning Teams* will be helpful. Begun at Good Shepherd Parish in Mount Vernon, Virginia, seven years ago and now operative in a dozen parishes, the Family Learning Team consists of approximately fifteen family units organized in geographical proximity to assume responsibility for the religious development of those families. Each family is put in the position of being a steward to the other fourteen families. In early September, the Family Learning Team comes together to decide which adults from their Family Learning Team will facilitate adult growth and teach their children this year, which adults will co-ordinate the team, and what day, time, and place will be best for meetings. All fifteen of these families volunteer their time, talents, house, etc., to the religious formation of the entire team. Beside providing adult education in the form of discussions, for example, the team concept provides the best environment for adult learning: learning for a purpose; learning for a value-laden task.

The Family Learning Team policy is based on the conclusion of the Greeley-Rossi report (1966) that no effective change in religious behavior is possible unless at least one parent is actively involved in the religious development of the child. In the Family Learning Teams this involvement is possible because each year a parent can choose to be a teacher, a host, a coordinator, a curriculum helper, or can take an active role in the Intergenerational Activity which is a culminating learning experience that involves all members of the Family Learning Team—adults and children. For example, one week each of the Family Learning Teams in the parish held intergenerational learning experiences that were the outgrowth of their previous three lessons and were entitled "Getting to Know You." Teams had liturgies, picnics, brunches, hikes, parties, where a puppet-making exercise facilitated their communal interaction and also played a part in the All Saints Family Liturgy. The Family Learning Team concept builds on healthy neighborhood community attitudes and tries to reconcile difficulties. Our experience has shown that the Family Learning Team structure brings problems of individuals and neighborhoods out into the open where we can then deal with them quickly, since willy-nilly the whole community educates the whole community, positively or negatively.

Parish as Collegial Subsidiarity

The view of parish which arises out of this approach to parish life as rooted in Roman Catholic tradition and derived from our pastoral experience can be described as collegial subsidiarity in practice. Parish, in this sense, is a living network of relationships that fully actualizes the universal church in a particular place. The local church is not only a part of the universal church, but it bears the qualities of the whole Church. "The Church of Christ is truly present in all legitimate local congregations of the faithful which, united with their pastors, are themselves called churches in the New Testament. For in their own locality these are the new people called by God, in the Holy Spirit and in much fullness" (see 1 Thessalonians 1:5).

The most intense actualization of the Church as event is in the celebration of the Eucharist. Since any given celebration must be by only one congregation in one place, the direction of the Church is toward this local actualization.

It follows that if the local eucharistic community is the universal church in miniature, then the basic principles of Church must be applied to parish structures. For instance, one of the most profound affirmations of Vatican II is the renewed emphasis on the Church as a collegial body. In describing the Church as the People of God, as a priestly people, as people equal in Baptism, the council fathers opened the door for the concepts of shared ministry and co-responsibility within the Church. They did not, however, close the door on a rigidly hierarchical ecclesiology. Consequently, we live in a church that Karl Rahner has aptly named the Church of non-simultaneity.[1]

The results are mixed. Without diversity or plurality of expressions we could not have grown so much in the past fifteen years. Nevertheless, the diversity can be a problem when different ecclesiologies clash. For example, the Dutch Church is quite different from the African Church, and this is good. Moreover, there is a healthy variety of expressions within one country. The plurality can be a problem, however, as is evident in Latin America, where the *communidades de base* co-exist with the monarchical style of the Church of the rich. Within our own country we witness radically divergent styles of authority from diocese to diocese. In one diocese the bishop lives in community, raising his own food, sharing decisions on all levels of Church life just as he shares the fruits of his garden. In another diocese the bishop's residence appears much like the protected palace of a Mid-East sultan. Even within each diocese the local churches differ. Some parishes operate out of a deep conviction of baptismal co-responsibility; others are unchanged in structure from 1950. One mobile Catholic whose job necessitates a move every three years said, "I feel like I'm in a time machine. For three years I endure incense and 'My dear children,' and for the next three years I'm badgered because I'm not running the Church."

Subsidiarity is another principle advocated by Vatican II. Coming from the Latin word meaning "aid" or "help," it has long been a focal principle of the Church's social teaching. Subsidiarity was defined clearly in Pius XI's Encyclical *Quadragesimo Anno:*

> It is indeed true, as history clearly proves, that owing to the change in social conditions, much that was formerly done by small bodies can nowadays be accomplished only by large corporations. Nonetheless, just as it is wrong to withdraw from the individual and commit to the community at large what private enterprise and industry can accomplish, so too is it an injustice, a grave evil and a disturbance of right order for a larger and higher organization to arrogate to itself functions which can be performed efficiently by smaller and lower bodies. This is a fundamental principle of social philosophy, unshaken and unchangeable, and it retains its full truth today. Of its very nature the true aim of all social activity should be to help individual

members of the social body, but never to destroy
or absorb. . . .

Let those in power, therefore, be convinced that
the more faithfully this principle be followed,
and a graded hierarchical order exists between
various subsidiary organizations, in observance of
the principle 'subsidiary function,' the more excellent will be both the authority and the effi-
ciency of the social organization as a whole and
the more prosperous the condition of the state.[2]

Pius XII, in a further development, applied subsidiarity to the structures of the Church,[3] and Vatican II
declared its approval of subsidiarity in *The Church in the
Modern World.*

Applying the principle of subsidiarity to the Church,
Hans Kung states:

The principle of subsidiarity requires that the
Petrine office leave to the bishops, priests, and
the people all that which can be carried out on
their own responsibility, whereby bishops,
priests, and people do not require the cooperation
of the Petrine office as such, and at the same time
it promotes the greatest possible participation in
the direction of the Church by bishops, priests,
and the people.[4]

According to William Bassett, Vatican II explicitly
removed the only serious canonical objection to subsidiarity
when it stated in the *Nota Praevia* (n. 2) that all previous
teachings must be reinterpreted in the light of the teaching
of the *Dogmatic Constitution on the Church.*[5] Hence it is
clear that the principle of subsidiarity can be and should be

applied to the ecclesial structure of the parish.

Family-Centered Catechesis

What are the basic assumptions of family-centered catechesis?

First, catechesis must nurture community, message, worship, and service primarily in the context of the relationships *within* a family, the smallest ecclesial unit. We are to be concerned with the real family-as-family: its story, its unique dynamic, its stage of development. In the family as a form of community, the other three elements—worship, message, and service—are already vitally present (*National Catechetical Directory*, n. 226) and in need of nurturing. The question then, is not how we can get parents to support the Catholic school or school-model CCD.

Centering catechesis in the family dynamic is consistent with the goals of the *PPAFM*[6] to develop the three ecclesial functions of the family: evangelizing, worshiping, and serving. Likewise, it is consistent with the *National Catechetical Directory*'s stress on family ministry as involving "announcing the good news to those within the immediate family circle first of all" (n. 226). What is paramount is the interpenetration of family and parish, not the question of what the parish can do for families or what families can do for the parish.

The second assumption of family-centered catechesis is that we must see the entire family unit as the Church in miniature (*National Catechetical Directory*, n. 226), with each member of the family sharing in a common baptismal ministry. We should ask not only how parents can catechize their children directly, which the *NCD* says is the ideal

(n. 226), but also how we can actualize each member within the family. The family grows because of the gifts that each member brings to the relationship in accordance with the diversity of the charisms given by the Spirit (see Ephesians 4:11-13).

> In a family which is conscious of this mission, all the members evangelize and are evangelized. The parents not only communicate the Gospel to their children, but from their children they can themselves receive the same Gospel as deeply lived by them. And such a family becomes the evangelizer of many other families, and of the neighborhood of which it forms part. (*On Evangelization*, Paul VI, n. 71; *National Catechetical Directory*, n. 226)

Therefore, family-centered catechesis suggests a broader focus than one which concerns itself exclusively with parents so that they can teach their children Scripture and doctrine. The type of community within the family, the depth of family prayer, and the social justice sense of the family are as vital to family-centered catechesis as is the learning/teaching component.

Thus, while the *NCD* assigns primacy to adult catechesis, it does not propose ministering to adults in isolation from their family or dealing exclusively with adults so that they can then impart doctrine to their children. That procedure would reinforce another pyramid model of the Church that is out of harmony with the community image so prevalent in the renewed ecclesiology of Vatican II and in subsequent documents. Rather, emphasis on adult catechesis is meant to insure that what is done at earlier stages is carried to its *culmination* in adulthood (*National*

Catechetical Directory, n. 188); it points to mature faith as the summit of the entire catechetical enterprise (*General Catechetical Directory*, n. 20).

Therefore, each member of the family community—young and old—is to be an active learner, worshiper, and server according to his/her particular roles and gifts. Every member of the family dynamic is a moving target, with change affecting the total family network. In fact, a total family-centered catechesis should develop a "scope and sequence" that nurtures the family and its changing needs as it passes through various stages of changes from the "no children" phase to the "empty nest" phase.

The third assumption is that family-centered catechesis is wholistic. It includes not only teaching, instruction, or message—the faith tradition—but also the nurturing of community, social justice, and prayer. Family-centered catechesis must include "both the message presented and the way in which it is presented" (*National Catechetical Directory*, n. 5).

In some circles, by contrast, people describe family-centered catechesis as including all aspects of religious nurturing except teaching the faith tradition. In this mindset "parents as primary religious educators of their children" is translated to mean, in reality, the responsibility of parents to send their children to Catholic schools or school-model CCD and to volunteer as catechists in such programs. In this view, family-centered catechesis functions as a sideshow to what is considered the main event, the real thing: school-model religious education.

However, a wholistic understanding of catechesis centering in families echoes the *NCD*'s comment that parents "catechize informally but powerfully by example and instruction" (n. 212). Even such *informal* instruction requires the parents to continue their own adult catechesis so that they can become confident in nurturing faith within their family. Further, parents can also *formally* catechize their children; when doing so, however, they "must be mindful of the pre-eminent right of the Church to specify the content of authentic catechesis" and must catechize accordingly (*National Catechetical Directory*, n. 212).

Family-centered catechesis demands, then, that we assist parents to catechize their children both formally and informally. The vision of the *PPAFM* and the *NCD* will facilitate structures that will enable family-centered catechesis to be effective. To some extent, a sufficient number of parents as resources are already available.

For example, Archbishop Jean Jadot stated recently that there are 168,000 Roman Catholic volunteer catechists in the United States who work with the elementary and secondary children and youth in parish programs. (This figure does not include people who teach in Catholic schools, in family life programs, in adult education, in preschools, or who are involved in youth ministry.) These 168,000 volunteers reach 8.4 million students, who represent a significant percentage of the families that compose the 50 million United States Catholics.

What happens if we look at these 168,000 adults as members of a family first rather than as catechists in parish programs? We then have a large number of families in which one member is already a formal catechizer outside the family. The Church can validate these adults to teach the faith within their family context and then to teach in inter-family or wider-based programs. In the future, sharing the faith at home would be the valued starting point for a "qualified" catechist; assisting the parents in their actual family situation would be the *sine qua non* for all "teacher training" programs; and demonstrating support for the parents' family system would be the focus of diocesan "certification" requirements.

In summary, when we view catechesis through the lens of family-centering, we see that the goals, resources, and personnel models of the parish catechetical ministry need restructuring. The underlying principle in this restructuring should be collegial subsidiarity. This means, first, that we should center catechesis *within* a family network rather than getting members of the family into programs modeled on the parish school. Second, all members of the family (not just parents), according to different roles and gifts, are to be mutually actualized in teaching. Third, formal and informal teaching of the faith tradition must be included in addition to community, social justice, and prayer within the family. Fourth, in a renewed family-centered catechesis, the parish catechist, the professional DRE, the pastor, the bishop, and the pope would have roles subsidiary to that of the parent/family: They would teach, enable, stimulate, and restrain as circumstances might suggest or necessity demand.

Family-centered catechesis does not of course eliminate the roles of professional and/or ordained ministries from the catechetical process. The bishop is still chief catechist in the diocese, responsible for seeing to it that sound catechesis is provided for all its people (*National Catechetical Directory*, n. 218). The pastor is still primarily responsible for seeing to it that the catechetical needs, goals, and priorities of the parish are identified and met (*National Catechetical Directory*, n. 217). Family-centered catechesis simply asks ministers to restructure their resources and time so that they can aid and support the family according to the roles and gifts of the family's members. Applying Pius XI's words on subsidiarity to the interrelation of ministries involved in family-centered catechesis, we could say: Let the Church be convinced that centering catechesis in the family will more faithfully apply the principle of subsidiarity and will improve the quality of both the local parish and the universal Church.

Family Learning Teams as a Model for the Local Church

So far in this essay we have advocated collegial subsidiarity as the basic structural component of co-responsibility in the parish. Secondly, we have proposed family-centered catechesis as a way to begin restructuring the parish according to this principle. By energizing the family—the small ecclesial community—to become more responsible in the catechetical mission of the Church, we really are influencing all people in the parish, since everyone comes from or lives in a family. Therefore, instead of dealing with parishioners only as individuals or in large groups, parishes would also nurture the family dynamic directly.

For the last seven years we have tested the validity of our suggestions by implementing Family Learning Teams in twelve parishes from Detroit to Tidewater, Virginia. In the light of this pastoral experience we now want to offer a practical catechetical model based on the Family Learning Teams structure.

We have already described Family Learning Teams as consisting of about fifteen households of faith (families) organized in geographical proximity to each other in order to assume responsibility for the team's religious development. The function of the parish staff is to act as resource, to encourage, and to assist in all ways the ministry of the team. They do this by providing curriculum, imparting a theological perspective, and facilitating communication—in short, by being generally helpful to the families who form the Family Learning Teams.

Our experience has been that the Family Learning Teams flourish when the priest and pastoral staff follow a servant model of authority. When the ministry within each team is not nurtured or supported, or when, for example, the parish is thought to revolve around the pastor, then the Family Learning Teams struggle and sometimes die. But when the ecclesial patterns enfleshed in Family Learning Teams are supported by compatible structures in the parish, the diocese, and the universal church, then the Family Learning Teams are seminal in restructuring the parish and diocese to better serve the people of God.

How could such a pastoral approach to parish life function? We propose the following plan.

1. All Catholic households within a fifteen-mile radius would be invited into geographical, neighborhood structures or into communal structures according to the principles of "base communities" (*communidades de base*). About thirty adults would be involved in each group. Adhering to the principle of collegial subsidiarity, these ecclesial communities would develop their gospel vision of Church according to the Church's tradition. Beginning with their individual and communal experience they would correlate their lived history with Christian texts and sources. For example, after identifying and sharing moments of alienation and reconciliation in their own lives,

they would reflect on the New Testament story of the prodigal son. In this way they could "live into" the message and spirit of Jesus from the bottom up.

2. All pastoral ministers from parishes within the fifteen-mile radius would be assembled into a wider, grassroots pastoral team. Each small ecclesial group could seek a member of this pastoral team to act as an animator and enabler so that the smaller group could implement their vision. If the members of the wider pastoral team could not match up with a small group, they could join a group as members, not as enablers, or could minister in another territory. If a small group could not decide upon an enabler from the pastoral team, they could either choose an animator from within their own group or seek one outside the zone.

3. These small groups should act on their vision and goals for two years as the animator attempts to develop the small community in *didache, diakonia,* and *koinonia* and to help them acquire the wider vision of the various zones of the diocese. Here we move from an emphasis on learning (Family Learning Teams) to total Church, with service, prayer, and community equally highlighted.

4. One or two of the existing parishes would be maintained, thus providing an established place of support and communication as well as allowing for diversity, since parishioners could choose to remain in these established parish structures. In addition, each small community would function as a local church—a mediating community—between the family and the wider Church structure. Just as the family is "the domestic Church" and the contemporary parish is the Church, so too these smaller teams of households would see themselves as Church.

Hence primary relationships could be nurtured within the small communities, while the continuity and availability of existing structures would provide stability to searchers.

Each mediating community would function according to the model of collegial subsidiarity in practice. The established place of support in each zone of the diocese would eventually consist of a network of these smaller communities. Together, they would compose the diocese. Functionally the diocese would provide a subsidiary service to these groups in the sense that it would aid the smaller units in their mission rather than substitute for them. In turn, all the mediating communities would gather as diocesan Church for Eucharist on the greater feasts. For example, at Easter they might gather at the civic coliseum with the bishop as celebrant.

5. These small ecclesial communities would therefore be connected with the wider territorial parishes, and thus with the diocese, according to the model of collegial subsidiarity in practice. The present diocese remains, but internally a major priority is given to the family as "domestic Church" and to the missing link between families and the wider parish—smaller mediating communities. Creating this realistic structure for a parish would allow it to truly be the Church actualized in a local eucharistic community.

Is such a plan practicable? We think so.

The Church needs pluralism and diversity within its communities, and there is already much evidence of changing parish structures. During the last fifteen years the "base communities" movement in such diverse places as France, Italy, Latin America, Africa, Quebec, and the United States has demonstrated people's great desire to experience Church in smaller ecclesial communities as an alternative

to parish life as it exists at present.[7] These "base communities" are just one example of collegial subsidiarity in
practice.

Another example is the sixty personal, non-territorial
parishes in over forty American dioceses studied by Robert
Lawrence. They reveal wide diversity of purposes,
membership, and responsibilities,[8] and the people involved
are seeking ecclesial experience in alternative ways to the
mainline territorial parishes. Some, such as the Genesis
Community in the diocese of Providence, have received
episcopal support, while others, such as Good Shepherd
Parish in the diocese of Arlington, Virginia, have had difficulties with their bishop.

Base communities, personal parishes, and, we might
add, Cursillo, Marriage Encounter, and Charismatic
Prayer Communities are all examples of parish according to
the proposed model. In fact, Bishop Albert Ottenweller
received an enthusiastic response at the November, 1975,
meeting of the National Catholic Conference of Bishops
when he called for the restructuring of the traditional parish along the line of smaller communities. He
maintains:

> Members of a parish have a need and a right to be
> like an extended family, to know each other, care
> for each other and so grow in love of God and of
> one another. My contention is that right now,
> organizationally, parishes are very heavy on in-
> stitution and very light on community. We think
> institution.[9]

At the bishops' meeting the next year, Archbishop Jean
Jadot, the Apostolic Delegate, told the bishops that they
must be willing to give greater responsibilities to the laity,

both men and women, as they together search for some new avenues of pastoral care.[10] The Family Learning Team does this.

Catechesis has a great potential as a catalyst for restructuring parishes according to the principle of collegial subsidiarity. First, the involvement of lay persons in the full-time religious education ministry of the United States Catholic Conference in dioceses and parishes is well established in the USA. Secondly, the actual experience of many lay persons sharing in the catechetical ministry as catechists and as other types of animators in the numerous parishes across the country has heightened awareness of the ability of lay persons to serve in all facets of Church life. Thirdly, the re-establishment of the parents as "the first and foremost catechists of their children" in theory and practice is taking hold in catechetical programs across the USA. Viewing parents as the primary catechists of their children clearly expresses a co-responsible ministry with the bishop and pastor.

Applying the principle of "collegial subsidiarity" to parish ministries would begin to eliminate the present false dichotomy of "clergy" and "laity." We ought not to begin our thinking of parish or local Church from either end of the continuum but should begin with the community, the People of God. After all, every Christian is "ecclesiastical," even if current ecclesiastical law books still speak with predilection of clerics as *"ecclesiastici."* Moreover, the ordained ministry arises *within* the ministry of the *laos*, the People of God, as an enabling ministry to equip, inspire, and deepen the faith of the people to carry out the primary ministry of the Church. The ordained minister is first of all a member of the *laos*.

Rosemary Reuther expresses the possibilities of "collegial subsidiarity in practice" as a model for approaching parish life:

> Ministry only resumes its proper function in the Church when it is defined from the bottom up, rather than from the top down; when it is defined from its foundations in the people and seen as arising out of the people, rather than defined in the platonic mode, which starts at the apex of the hierarchy (as a level "closest to God") and then trickles down to the lower levels until it finally reaches the people, as the "lowest level of reality." Such a platonic concept of a hierarchically derived ministry is actually anti-incarnational.[11]

In our model, laity and priest share equally in the ministry of the Church. Each is involved in co-responsible decision-making on all levels of Church life. Priests share in the temporal mission of the Church according to their vocation and personal charism. Laypersons share in the whole mission of the Church—in its ecclesial structure and in the world—according to their vocation and personal charism. Neither should be limited to the "spiritual" or the "temporal" order but together should carry out the more universal mission of the *laos*, the People of God.

As a pastoral approach to the parish, our model would allow the "church of non-simultaneity" to be sensitively ministered to. Also, it would be aware of the tension and conflict inherent in ecclesial communities structured "from below." All in all, it would help the People of God be more clearly "servant of the servants of God."

Notes

1. *The Shape of the Church to Come* (New York: Seabury Press, 1972), p. 35.
2. In *Acta Apostolicae Sedis* 23 (1931):203; also quoted by John XXIII in *Mater et Magistra* and referred to in the *Pastoral Constitution on the Church in the Modern World*, n. 86.
3. "Address to the Newly Appointed Cardinals," in *Acta Apostolicae Sedis* 38 (1946):14.
4. *Structures of the Church* (New York: Thomas Nelson & Sons, 1964), p. 242.
5. "Subsidiarity, Order and Freedom in the Church," *The Once and Future Church* (Staten Island: Alba House, 1971), pp. 245-46. For detailed references to subsidiarity in Vatican II documents, see pp. 249-59.
6. The recommendations on family contained in the 1976 Call to Action Conference in Detroit led to *The Plan of Pastoral Action for Family Ministry: A Vision and Strategy (PPAFM)* approved by the U.S. bishops in May 1978.
7. Thomas G. Bissonnette, "Communidades Ecclesiales de Base: Some Contemporary Attempts to Build Koinonia," *The Jurist* 36 (1976):24-58.
8. Robert Lawrence, *Membership and Accompanying Responsibilities in Non-Territorial Parishes in the United States* (Washington, D.C.: The Catholic University of America Press, 1974), pp. 218-22.
9. Bishop Albert Ottenweller, "A Call to Restructure the Parish," *Origins* 5 (1975):395.

10.   Archbishop Jean Jadot, "Signs of the Times/Pastoral Problems," *Origins* 6 (1976):356.
11.   "The Ministry of the Laity," *Notre Dame Journal of Education* 5 (1974):71.

For Further Reading

Developing Basic Christian Communities: A Handbook. Chicago: National Federation of Priests' Councils, 1979.

Family-Centered Catechesis: Guidelines and Resources. Washington, D.C.: USCC Publications Office, 1979.

Family Ministry: Diocesan Implementation. Washington, D.C.: USCC Publications Office, 1979.

Fenhagen, James. *Mutual Ministry.* New York: Seabury Press, 1977.

Kilian, Sabbas. *Theological Models of the Parish.* New York: Alba House, 1976.